NEW JERUSALEM LUTHERAN CHURCH CEMETERY

NEW JERUSALEM LUTHERAN CHURCH
EST. 1765
LOVETTSVILLE, VIRGINIA

Marty Hiatt, CG
and
Craig R. Scott, CG, FUGA

HERITAGE BOOKS
2019

HERITAGE BOOKS
AN IMPRINT OF HERITAGE BOOKS, INC.

Books, CDs, and more—Worldwide

For our listing of thousands of titles see our website
at
www.HeritageBooks.com

Published 2019 by
HERITAGE BOOKS, INC.
Publishing Division
5810 Ruatan Street
Berwyn Heights, Md. 20740

Church drawing on cover by Robin Tatina.

International Standard Book Number
Paperbound: 978-1-888265-05-7

Introduction

The New Jerusalem Lutheran congregation was established in 1765 by people who were predominately of a rural German background. Soon after a church building was constructed, burials began around it. Today's church and cemetery occupy a triangular area of approximately 12 acres. New Jerusalem Cemetery is adjacent to the Lovettsville Union Cemetery, however, separation between the two is easily discernible from behind the church building.

There are many unmarked graves, so the earliest burial is not known. The earliest readable inscription if that of Isack Vckens (sic) 1770. There are a few stones from the 1780s and 1790s, but by far the vast majority date from the 1800s. The oldest stones are in the back, surrounding an open space where the old church once stood.

Over the years several stones have been removed, reset, or have sunk completely out of sight. Mrs. Aurelia Jewell copied information from the headstones in 1949, when the cemetery was badly overgrown and neglected. Pastor Michael Kretsinger led the drive to clean up the cemetery in 1959, at which time additional headstone information was added to Mrs. Jewell's list. A comparison of her list with today's list demonstrates two facts: 1) Some of the stones she transcribed are no longer present, or have deteriorated to an illegible state, and 2) Seventy eight stones which Mrs. Jewell did not record have been "found" and their information is included in this book.

Still, this is not a complete listing of everyone buried in the New Jerusalem Cemetery. The Lutheran pastors began recording burials in 1785, and those registers list burials for many people who do not have headstones, or are not buried here. As one walks through the cemetery is it obvious that there are many unmarked graves, and the outlines of several sunken stones are visible. It is the hope of New Jerusalem to establish a fund to repair and restore headstones in this cemetery.

This book is organized in three parts. First, is an alphabetical list, followed by a row order list, then an index for names other than the decedents. Organizing and arranging the row order list was difficult. From the front of the cemetery, near the church, the rows appear to be in neat order, running from north to south. As one walks towards the back of the cemetery the rows stop and start in different places, zig-zag, and curve.

There are stones which stand alone, or with one or two others, in between well defined rows. In some cases there is a space of 50 to 100 feet between stones. Whether this spacing was intentional, or stones sunk into the ground, or have been removed, is not known. The boundaries of family plots are seldom discernible. While some family members will be found next to each other in a row, others are located in front or back of each other, in different rows.

Narrative inscriptions were not copied from the stones. Information that was copied includes full names, date, and relationships, when stated. The notation "fieldstone," indicates a non-commercial stone was used to mark a grave. It may, or may not have an inscription. When it was difficult to decipher information on a headstone, Mrs. Jewell's list was consulted, and data taken from it. We believe that it may have been easier to read the stones fifty years ago. In some instances, a stone which is completely illegible today could be determined by comparing its location to the earlier list. If we were certain, the data was copied from Mrs. Jewell. If there was a question, the stone was marked "illegible."

Several footstones, and a few headstones, have been removed from their original places. These were stacked in a pile at the back of the cemetery. The headstones have been removed from the pile and are now visible, but certainly not in their original locations. Instead of having a row number, these stones are listed as "Pile," and will be found at the back (east end) of the cemetery.

Finally, we included information from stones which Mrs. Jewell recorded, but were not found by the compliers in 1994. These stones are identified as "List."

A portion of the proceeds from the sale of this book will go the to the New Jerusalem Lutheran Church Cemetery Restoration Fund. Individuals who are interested in contributing additional money to this fund, may mail their tax deductable gift to: New Jerusalem Lutheran Church, Cemetery Restoration Fund, P. O. Box 210, Lovettsville, Virginia 22080.

Marty Hiatt, CGRS
Craig R. Scott, CGRS, FSA Scot
Rt. 1, Box 15A
Lovettsville, Virginia 22080
March 1995

To find a stone

1) Locate the name of interest in the alphabetical listing. Note the alpha numeric
   designation for the row and stone.

2) Use the letters (A-UU) to find the row. Walk along the fence, going away
   from the church, until the row is located.

3) Use the number to find the stone in that row. You will have to read right-to-left, as the numbers begin somewhere near the fence, or at least on that side of the cemetery.

The most difficult rows to locate will be the short ones that begin across the field, or on the north side of the cemetery. Most stones face west, but a few are turned to the east. Always look on both sides of every headstone.

Some very old, scattered stones are in the back, southeast corner of the cemetery. They have been identified as "OO" in the list, but are not arranged in a row.

If you plan a trip to Lovettsville to read and photograph this cemetery, the best time of day is late afternoon. The majority of stones are most readable between 2:00 p.m. and 4:00 p.m.

ALPHABETICAL LIST

QQ 2   ALDER, Albert, b. 4 Apr 1811, d. 22 Feb 1864 at 49y 10m 18d.

UU 12   ALDER, Sarah C., consort of George W. ALDER, b. 12 Mar 1834, d. 13 Aug 1862 at 28y 5m.

UU 13   ALDER, Wm. R., son of George W. & Sarah ALDER, b. 30 Mar 1862, d. 22 Oct 1862.

II 15   AMRY, Adam, son of Jacob AMRY, Dec'd, d. 26 Jun 1813 at 28y 2w.

II 14   AMRY, John, son of Jacob AMRY, d. 27 Jun 1803 at 20y 7m 13d.

J 17   ARNOLD, Charles W., d. 8 Aug 1882 at 27 yrs.

N 4   ARNOLD, David, b. 21 Sep 1814, d. 6 Jul 1842 at 27y 9m 15d.

I 4   ARNOLD, Elizabeth P., consort of John ARNOLD, d. 29 Apr 1859 at 39y 1m 15d.

MM 1   ARNOLD, Estella V., daughter of Noah & Emeline ARNOLD, b. 14 Aug 1843, d. 18 Oct 1865
        at 22 yrs.

H 8   ARNOLD, Jacob, d. 5 Oct 1861 at 74 yrs.

I 15   ARNOLD, John, b. 5 Aug 1816, d. 1 Jan 1902.

F 3   ARNOLD, Joseph, b. 4 Dec 1819, d. 12 Dec 1878.

E 2   ARNOLD, Martha A., wife of Joseph ARNOLD, d. 26 Jun 1880 at 74 yrs.

L 1   ARNOLD, Martin L., b. 10 Sep 1820, d. 13 Feb 1853 at 32y 5m 3d.

H 9   ARNOLD, Mary, wife of Jacob ARNOLD, d. 28 Jan 1865 at 71y 2m 28d.

R 10   ARNOLD, Michael, d. 11 May 1863 at 72y 8m 5d.

N 3   ARNOLD, Noah, b. 27 Apr 1817, d. 7 Jun 1850 at 33y 1m 10d.

N 5   ARNOLD, Sophia Matilda, daughter of Noah & Emiline ARNOLD, b. 14 Oct 1841,
        d. 31 Aug 1854 at 12y 10m 17d.

X 4   AULT, Rachel, d. 25 Aug 1834 at 68y 3m 18d.

V 6   AUMEN, Barbara, d. 17 Aug 1832 at 60y 8m 15d.

GG 10   AUMEN, Rebecca, daughter of Lawrence AUMEN, d. 22 Mar 1826 at 23y 11m 11d.

GG 7   AUMENT, George, son of Lawrence AUMENT, b. 1788, d. 24 Apr 1819 at 31y 8m 4d.

GG 8   AUMENT, Lawrence, husband of Barbara, d. 13 Feb 1814 at 50y 3w 3d.

GG 9   AUMENT, Moley, wife of Antney AUMAN, d. 16 Dec 1806 at 40y 1m 1d.

L 9   AXLINE, Catharine S., consort of David AXLINE, b. 27 Nov 1816, d. 24 Nov 1849 at
        32y 11m 27d.

AA 3   AXLINE, Christina, wife of John AXLINE, d. 16 Apr 1828 at 78 yrs.

L 6   AXLINE, David, b. 17 Feb 1772, d. 9 Nov 1844 at 72y 8m 22d.

L 7   AXLINE, Eve, wife of David AXLINE, b. 6 May 1776, d. 4 Jul 1854.

HH 1   AXLINE, George, son of Jacob AXLINE, d. 16 Jun 1803 at 1y 1d.

S 15   AXLINE, Gideon, son of John AXLINE, d. 17 Nov 1826 at 7y 10m 20d.

T 20   AXLINE, Harriet A., wife of David AXLINE, b. 9 Jan 1819, d. 17 Nov 1867.

R 5   AXLINE, Henry Harrison, son of Emanuel & Susan AXLINE, d. 29 Aug 1840, d. 7 Nov 1846 at
         6y 2m 8d.

MM 5   AXLINE, John W., son of David E. & Martha AXLINE. [no dates]

AA 2   AXLINE, John, d. 19 Feb 1833 at 93y 5m. [D.A.R. Marker]

S 13   AXLINE, Samuel V., son of Emanuel AXLINE, d. 3 Sep 1838 at 4y 2m 12d.

T 21   AXLINE, Sarah Jane, wife of David AXLINE, b. 14 Apr 1877 at 35y 20d.

S 12   AXLINE, Silas A., d. 13 Mar 1838 at 15m.

S 14   AXLINE, William T., son of Emanuel & Susannah AXLINE, d. 3 Aug 1829 at 5y 3m 17d.

T 6   AXLINE, William T., son of Emmanuel & Susannah AXLINE, d. 21 Aug 1829 at 8y 3m 12d.

FF 4   BAKER, Elizabeth, daughter of William BAKER, d. 17 Apr 1808 at 10m 6d.

M 7   BARTLETT, Adah Virginia, daughter of Nathaniel & Margaret BARTLETT, b. 26 Dec 1868,
         d. 23 Aug 1870.

Q 13   BARTLETT, Alice M., daughter of John W. & Elizabeth BARTLETT, d. 18 Aug 1867 at
         2m 27d.

X 10   BARTLETT, Elizabeth H., b. 17 Jun 1835, d. 9 Feb 1872 at 36y 7m 23d.

R 6   BEAMER, Infant son of James W. & Mary Elizabeth BEAMER, b. 23 Oct 1853, d. 9 Nov 1853
         at 15d.

K 11   BEAMER, Julia Ann, wife of Michael BEAMER, b. 16 Jun 1815, d. 20 Oct 1852 at 27y 4m 4d.

K 12   BEAMER, Mary Elizabeth, wife of James W. BEAMER, d. 19 Nov 1853 at 22y 2m 2d.

Q 6   BEAMER, Peter, son of Geo. & Catharine BEAMER, b. 22 Jan 1821, d. 8 Jul 1845 at 21y 5m 16d.

S 11   BELSO, Frederic, d. 19 Jan 1831 at 88 yrs.

PP 2   BEST, Albert, b. 7 Jan 1807, d. 22 Feb 1864 at 57y 1m 15d.

PP 11   BEST, Elizabeth, d. 18 Mar 1894 at 84y 2m 14d.

II 4   BOGER, Frederick, b. 7 Feb 1752, d. 16 Oct 1791 at 39y 2m 2w 4d.

UU 4   BOGER, James, b. 10 Feb 1799, d. 24 Jun 1871.

UU 11   BOGER, John, b. 24 Sep 1801, d. 29 Jan 1862.

UU 7   BOGER, Mary A., d. 14 Dec 1876 at 60y 9m.

UU 5   BOGER, Mary E., daughter of Jacob & Mary BOGER, b. 20 Oct 1869, d. 9 Mar 1870.

L 22   BOGER, Mary E., daughter of Samuel & Mary BOGER, b. 25 Jun 1854, d. 4 Aug 1857 at
        3y 1m 9d.

CC 4   BOGER, Mary Elizabeth, b. 27 Jul 1761, d. 13 Dec 1813 at 79y 1m 17d.

CC 3   BOGER, Michael, b. 1 Apr 1762, d. 26 Mar 1822 at 59y 11m 1d.

Pile   BOGER, Peter, d. 19 Feb 1790 [Broken - German inscription]

UU 6   BOGER, Philip, d. 16 Jun 1865 at 76y 11m 1d.

UU 8   BOGER, Samuel L., b. 5 Feb 1806, d. 30 Jun 1867 at 61y 4m 25d.

UU 3   BOGER, Sarah C., daughter of S. & M. BOGER, d. 13 Oct 1878 at 12y 11m.

RR 16   BOWERS, John H., b. 13 Dec 1820, d. 23 Feb 1880 at 59y 2m 10d.

SS 2   BOWERS, Mary A., wife of John H. BOWERS, b. 24 Aug 1823, d. 3 Jan 1868.

LL 9   BRAMHALL, Blanco W., b. 29 Feb 1828, d. 26 May 1903.

LL 10   BRAMHALL, Rebecca J., b. 7 Oct 1836, d. 11 Nov 1910.

JJ 4   BRAMHALL, Robert, b. 26 Nov 1871, d. 8 Jan 1906.

UU 2   BRAMHALL, Walter E., son of Blanco W. & R. J. BRAMHALL, b. 10 Sep 1864, d. 9 Aug 1865
        at 10m 30d.

List   BROOKS, Iva, d. 17 Oct 1936 at 19 yrs.

CC 6   C. E. A. [fieldstone]

KK 17   C. M. F. 1803.

NN 13   CARNES, Marietta, wife of Abram E. CARNES, d. 7 Sep 1865 at 24y 8m 27d.

JJ 1   CARNES, Silas C., son of Samuel L. & Sarah M. CARNES, b. 28 May 1854, d. 17 Nov 1866 at
        11y 11m 20d.

K 22   CASE, Mabel Amelia, daughter of G. W. & Rose CASE, d. 4 Jul 1890 at 11m 5d.

Y 1   CEMPHER, John W., infant son of Saml. & H. CEMPHER, d. 26 Jan 1844 at 9d.

S 3   COLLINS, Margaret A., d. 30 Oct 1888 at 76y 3m 5d.

H 5   COMPHER, Anna C. Kadel, wife of Peter COMPHER, b. 28 May 1785, d. 9 Oct 1860.

J 4   COMPHER, Anna Mary, wife of William COMPHER, and daughter of Henry & Christina
        FAWLEY, b. 6 Sep 1814, d. 20 Sep 1854.

RR 15   COMPHER, Charles C., son of John H. & Margaret A. COMPHER, b. 16 Oct 1864,
                 d. 10 Jul 1865 at 8m 24d.

U 16   COMPHER, Christena, daughter of William & M. COMPHER, b. 12 Nov 1845, d. 1 Jun 1846
                 at 6m 20d.

CC 12   COMPHER, Cora V., daughter of William F. & Sarah C. COMPHER, b. 31 May 1873,
                 d. 15 Sep 1874 at 1y 3m 15d.

CC 15   COMPHER, Dasie N., daughter of F. & J. COMPHER, b. 22 Jan 1875.

RR 11   COMPHER, Ebenezer N., son of John & Elizabeth M. COMPHER, d. 4 Nov 1863 at 7y 15d.

X 6   COMPHER, Elizabeth Almira, only daughter of Joseph & Susannah COMPHER,
                 d. 14 Jun 1865 at 15y 1m 20d.

P 16   COMPHER, Esther Ann, consort of John COMPHER, b. 2 Sep 1823, d. 25 Sep 1846 at 23y 23d.

KK 24   COMPHER, Hannah, wife of Samuel COMPHER, daughter of Israel & Amelia WILLIAMS,
                 b. 1 Dec 1817, d. 1 Sep 1868 at 38 y 9m.

List   COMPHER, Jessie W., daughter of John & Elizabeth M. COMPHER, d. 16 Jan 1861 at
                 4y 8m 28d.

UU 15   COMPHER, John, b. 11 Apr 1806, d. 12 Oct 1862 at 59y 6m 1d.

HH 4   COMPHER, John, Sr., b. 16 Oct 1740, d. 26 Mar 1815 at 75y 5m 10d.

S 1   COMPHER, John, Sr., b. 4 Dec 1773, d. 24 Apr 1846 at 72y 4m 20d.

W 16   COMPHER, Margaret, wife of Peter COMPHER, b. 13 Jan 1786, d. 11 Sep 1867 at 81y 8m.

HH 5   COMPHER, Maria Cathren, wife of John COMPHER, Sr., b. 4 Feb 1755, d. 14 Mar 1815 at
                 60 yrs.

R 8   COMPHER, Mariah E., wife of John COMPHER, d. 19 May 1862 at 77y 9m 22d.

J 3   COMPHER, Mary, daughter of John & Elizabeth COMPHER, b. 20 Sep 1810, d. 29 Oct 1854
                 at 44y 1m 9d.

KK 25   COMPHER, Milly Ann, daughter of Samuel & Hannah COMPHER, b. 15 Mar 1842,
                 d. 10 Mar 1867 at 24y 11m 25d.

W 17   COMPHER, Peter, b. 21 May 1793, d. 3 Mar 1886 at 92y 9m 12d.

HH 6   COMPHER, Peter, b. 24 Aug 1776, d. 5 Nov 1858 at 82y 2m 12d.

K 6   COMPHER, Samuel Edward, son of Wm. & E. COMPHER, b. 28 Jun 1854, d. 17 Sep 1854 at
                 2m 19d.

KK 27   COMPHER, Samuel, b. 8 Oct 1818, d. 26 Mar 1883.

P 15   COMPHER, Sarah, d. 24 Apr 1842 at 5 yrs.

UU 1   COMPHER, Susan, b. 25 Sep 1810, d. 23 Oct 1879 at 69y 28d.

HH 7   COMPHER, Susanna, wife of Peter COMPHER, b. 12 Mar 1779, d. 5 Apr 1815 at 36y 3w 3d.

KK 28   COMPHER, Ulysses S., son of Jonas J. & Mary C. COMPHER, b. 18 Oct 1866, d. 18 Aug 1868 at
        1y 9m 21d.

K 6   COMPHER, William, b. 3 Feb 1812, d. 16 Sep 1854.

T 8   CONRAD, Mary Catherine, daughter of Abner & Mary C. CONRAD, d. 17 Feb 1841 at
        2m 27d.

V 2   COOPER, Aaron, d. 13 Dec 1878 at 61y 2m 25d.

T 16   COOPER, Adam, d. 28 Jun 1890 at 79y 8m 3d.

HH 2   COOPER, Ann Catharine [no date] at 21y 2m 5d.

CC 10   COOPER, Annie E., b. 30 Mar 1843, d. 2 Dec 1872 at 29y 8m 2d.

B 2   COOPER, Benjamin F., b. 13 Jun 1856, d. 26 Dec 1917.

Z 5   COOPER, Clara Esther, daughter of George & Mary C. COOPER, b. 11 Oct 1854,
        d. 3 Sep 1855 at 10m 23d.

N 14   COOPER, Elizabeth E., wife of Philip COOPER, b. 4 Mar 1777, d. 30 Jul 1863 at 86y 4m 26d.

Z 2   COOPER, Elizabeth Jane, daughter of George & Mary C. COOPER, b. 6 Sep 1850,
        d. 9 Apr 1851 at 7m 3d.

NN 12   COOPER, Elizabeth, daughter of John & Eve Ann COOPER, b. 9 Nov 1811, d. 9 Jun 1865 at
        53y 7m.

E 7   COOPER, Emeline, b. 18 Apr 1818, d. 1 Jun 1881 at 63y 1m 13d.

B 1   COOPER, Esther V., b. 19 Aug 1850, d. 9 Jun 1906.

J 9   COOPER, Eve Ann, wife of John COOPER, b. 29 Mar 1882, d. 28 Apr 1856 at 71y 30d.

BB 4   COOPER, Frederick, d. 29 Apr 1825 at 58 yrs.

FF 14   COOPER, George F., d. 19 Aug 1894 at 63y 10m 6d.

S 4   COOPER, George F., son of Fredrick C. COOPER, b. 6 Aug 1792, d. 25 Aug 1833 at 41y 19d.

N 16   COOPER, George, b. 14 Feb 1770, d. 18 Aug 1846 at 76y 6m 4d.

D 4   COOPER, George, b. 9 Mar 1820, d. 16 Dec 1892.

AA 7   COOPER, Harry E., son of George & Mary C. COOPER, d. 3 Oct 1880 at 6y 8m 4d.

FF 13   COOPER, Henry C., d. 19 Dec 1888 at 56y 2m 25d.

L 15   COOPER, Henry Clay, son of John & Sarah COOPER, b. 9 Dec 1844. [no death date]

RR 8   COOPER, John, son of George & Mary COOPER, b. 1 Aug 1797, d. 12 Dec 1863 at 66y 4m 11d.

J 11   COOPER, John, Sr., b. 29 Feb 1782, d. 10 Nov 1856 at 74y 8m 10d.

UU 17   COOPER, Joseph, son of William F. & Lydia E. COOPER, 27 May 1856, d. 25 Aug 1863.

I 9   COOPER, Julius Tilghman, b. 10 Oct 1852, d. 23 Jan 1860.

Z 4   COOPER, Lydia E., daughter of G. & M. C. COOPER, d. 24 Feb 1864 at 8d.

UU 16   COOPER, Lydia E., wife of William F. COOPER, d. 29 Dec 1862 at 35yrs.

V 2   COOPER, Margaret, d. 16 Jan 1918 at 91yrs.

W 6   COOPER, Mary A., wife of Michael L. COOPER, d. 25 Sep 1896 at 73y 3m 17d.

D 4   COOPER, Mary C., wife of George COOPER, b. 24 Mar 1833, d. 1 Jan 1897.

S 2   COOPER, Mary E., wife of Adam COOPER, b. 25 May 1833, d. 10 Jan 1892.

T 15   COOPER, Mary J., wife of Adam COOPER, d. 10 Nov 1864 at 50y 7m.

B 3   COOPER, Mary S., b. 5 Jun 1856, d. 9 Dec 1932.

Z 3   COOPER, Mary Virginia, daughter of George & Mary Catharine COOPER, b. 1 Nov 1852,
        d. 6 Nov 1852 at 6d.

N 15   COOPER, Mary, wife of George COOPER, b. 12 Aug 1774, d. 16 Feb 1858 at 83y 6m 4d.

W 5   COOPER, Michael L., d. 18 May 1884 at 85y 5m 22d.

N 11   COOPER, Philip, b. 8 Oct 1775, d. 13 Jun 1843 at 67y 8m 5d.

FF 15   COOPER, Sarah J., d. 16 Sep 1914 at 82 yrs.

J 6   COOPER, Solomon, b. 8 Nov 1803, d. 2 Aug 1855 at 51y 8m.

J 18   COOPER, son of R. H. & A. P. COOPER

A 1   COOPER, Thomas J., b. 4 Nov 1853, d. 12 Apr 1918.

UU 18   COOPER, William F., son of William F. & Lydia E. COOPER, b. 23 Sep 1854, d. 11 Sep 1863.

L 14   COOPER, William Washington, son of John & Sarah COOPER, b. 7 Jan 1831, d. 26 Jun 1845 at
        14y 5m 19d.

GG 1   COOPPER, Adam, son of Phillip COOPPER, 4 Sep — [illegible]

HH 3   COOPPER, Michael, Sr., b. 20 Jun 1742, d. 19 Feb 1815 at 72y 7m 3w 6d.

I 15   COPELAND, Mary C., b. 18 Feb 1846, d. 20 Mar 1909.

NN 5   CORDELL, America Virginia, daughter of John & Sarah Ann CORDELL, b. 13 Aug 1851,
        d. 2 Apr 1855 at 7m 19d.

LL 2   CORDELL, Susan, wife of Adam CORDELL, daughter of Jacob & Catharine SLATER,
        b. 27 May 1809, d. 18 Jun 1853 at 44y 22d.

U 17   CRIM, Catharine A. E., daughter of John H. & Mary M. CRIM, d. 22 Mar 1852 at 1y 6d.

Y 2   CRIM, Charles, d. 17 Sep 1824 at 80y 11m 18d.

U 18   CRIM, George P., son of John H. & Mary M. CRIM, d. 18 Aug 1865 at 18y 6m 12d.

T 12   CRIM, Jacob, b. 26 Dec 1772, d. 22 May 1847 at 74y 4m 26d.

Pile   CRIM, John H., b. 12 Feb 1816, d. 5 Oct 1879 at 63 yrs.

U 15   CRIM, Margaret, wife of John CRIM, b. 5 Feb 1798, d. 8 Sep 1834 at 36y 6m 3d.

U 23   CRIM, Mary M., wife of John H. CRIM, d. 18 Sep 1865 at 43y 4m 5d.

NN 7   CRIM, Rosanah, wife of Abraham CRIM, b. 21 Feb 1780, d. 8 Oct 1865 at 85y 7m 15d.

D 1   CRIM, Susan C., wife of Armistead CRIM, d. 28 Aug 1890 at 54y 5m 11d.

U 3   CRIM, Susannah, b. 5 Jan 1790, d. 2 Jun 1857.

MM 2   CRUMBAKER, Elizabeth, daughter of Solomon & Catharine CRUMBAKER, b. 10 Jul 1813,
           d. 10 Oct 1870.

MM 4   CRUMBAKER, Annie C., b. 22 Aug 1787, d. 9 Oct 1866 at 79y 1m 17d.

MM 3   CRUMBAKER, Solomon, b. 25 Jul 1784, d. 8 Jan 1866 at 81y 5m 13d.

OO 3   DAVIS, Esther, b. – Aug 1750, d. 16 Sep 1795 at 45y 1m.

List   DAVIS, George, son of Jacob & Susan DAVIS, b. 6 Oct 1810, d. 28 Oct 1821 at 11y 22d.

T 5   DERRY, Eliza, wife of Peter DERRY, d. 16 Mar 1827 at 25 yrs.

I 15   DONALDSON, Robert B., b. 7 Apr 1878, d. 31 Aug 1910.

I 15   DONALDSON, Walter S., b. 1 Jan 1829, d. 23 Nov 1884.

TT 9   DOWNEY, Amanda K., daughter of J. M. & A. E. DOWNEY, 13 Jan 1861 at 24 yrs.

TT 3   DOWNEY, Annie E., b. 3 Jun 1812, d. 16 Mar 1881 at 68y 11m 13d.

TT 1   DOWNEY, Calvin Welty, d. 26 Mar 1885 at 30y 11m 22d.

TT 2   DOWNEY, J. M., b. 12 Dec 1809, d. 28 Mar 1881 at 71y 3m 16d.

TT 6   DOWNEY, John F., son of J. M. & A. E. DOWNEY, d. 1 Apr 1862 at 23 yrs. in the service of
           country.

TT 8   DOWNEY, Leila B., daughter of J. M. & A. E. DOWNEY, 2 Jan 1865 at 17 yrs.

TT 7   DOWNEY, Rose J., daughter of J. M. & A. E. DOWNEY, 7 Aug 1867 at 17 yrs.

TT 4   DOWNEY, W. Scott, d. 12 Feb 1878 at 30y 9m 1d.

TT 5   DOWNEY, William Burns, d. 9 Mar 1873 at 37 yrs.

Q 9   EAMICH, John, b. Apr 1783, d. 7 Jan 1845 at 62y 9m.

Q 10   EDWARDS, George W., son of Thomas M. & Sarah EDWARDS, b. 20 Mar 1861, d. 16 Jun 1862
           at 1y 2m 26d.

Q 11   EDWARDS, Jonathan, d. 5 Apr 1873 at 41y 3m 12d.

II 16   EMERY, Catharine, wife of Jacob EMERY, d. 27 Mar 1834 at about 72 yrs.

II 17   EMERY, Jacob, d. 29 Oct 1815 at 71y 9m.

List   ENGLISH, Archibald, son of William T. & L. Maud ENGLISH, b. 21 Sep 1865, d. 15 Dec 1865
        at 2m 26d.

C 3   ENGLISH, Ellen O., b. 16 Mar 1847, d. 22 Jun 1917.

L 25   ENGLISH, Hauer Chester, son of W. T. & E. O. ENGLISH, b. 21 Jan 1872 at 9d.

L 26   ENGLISH, Lucy E., infant of W. T. & E. O. ENGLISH, d. 24 Jun 1890.

C 4   ENGLISH, William T., b. 21 Jun 1840, d. 13 Aug 1912.

KK 8   EVERHART, Ann Elizabeth, daughter of Jacob & Sarah EVERHART, d. 6 Jan 1830 at
        2y 1d. [broken]

P 7   EVERHART, Christina, wife of Michael EVERHART, d. 18 Jun 1846 at 66y 7m 18d.

J 15   EVERHART, Eliza A., d. 11 Feb 1857 at 40y 16d.

T 14   EVERHART, J., son of John & S. EVERHART, d. 4 Jun – at 3d.

KK 9   EVERHART, Jacob, b. 3 Feb 1796, d. 23 Nov 1828.

II 5   EVERHART, Lydia, wife of Joseph EVERHART, d. 13 Apr 1830 at 24y 8m 15d.

P 6   EVERHART, Michael, b. 29 Sep 1772, d. 14 Jan 1853.

KK 7   EVERHART, Mortimer, son of Jacob EVERHART, d. 11 May 1826 at 3m 18d.

O 3   EVERHART, Susan Manzilla, daughter of John & Mary E. EVERHART, b. 12 Sep 1853,
        d. 26 Aug 1854.

QQ 4   EVERHART, William F., b. 3 Jul 1844, d. 10 Aug 1864 at 20y 1m 7d.

II 13   FAWLEY, Anna Maria, wife of John FAWLEY, d. 2 Oct 1803 at 66 yrs.

I 11   FAWLEY, Christena, wife of Henry FAWLEY, b. 18 May 1786, d. 9 Jan 1861 at 74y 7m 21d.

List   FAWLEY, Florence May, daughter of Joseph & Ann C. FAWLEY, b. 2 May 1853, d. 2 Sep 1856
        at 3y 4m.

W 13   FAWLEY, George, b. 4 Feb 1804, d. 1 Jan 1815 at 10y 11m 11d.

LL 1   FAWLEY, Henry Washington, son of Joseph & Catherine FAWLEY, b. 17 Jan 1849,
        d. 11 Jul 1851 at 2y 5m 24d.

I 10   FAWLEY, Henry, b. 4 Mar 1784, d. 2 Jul 1860 at 76y 3m 28d.

W 12   FAWLEY, Jacob, d. 20 Mar 1843 at 82 yrs.

II 12   FAWLEY, John, d. 11 Jun 1803 at 83y 5m 11d.

N 10   FAWLEY, John, d. 15 July 1850 at 89y 10m 3d.

P 1   FAWLEY, Margaret, wife of John FAWLEY, d. at 76 yrs.

UU 19   FAWLEY, Sally Ann, daughter of John & Mary FAWLEY, b. 12 Oct 1858, d. 10 Dec 1862 at 4y 1m 29d.

M 2   FAWLEY, Sally Gertrude, daughter of William & Elizabeth FAWLEY, b. 30 Nov 1856, d. 23 Dec 1859 at 3y 23d.

M 3   FAWLEY, Sarah E., daughter of William & Elizabeth FAWLEY, b. 2 Apr 1842, d. 1 Aug 1845.

R 1   FILLER, Henry, b. 12 Dec 1801, d. 22 Jul 1831 at 29y 7m 10d.

J 5   FRY, Andrew, b. 20 Oct 1790, d. 12 Aug 1854 at 63y 21m 11d.

G 2   FRY, Angeline, b. 27 Jul 1824, d. 6 Mar 1875.

U 1   FRY, C. Catharine, wife of G. H. FRY, d. 16 Mar 1897 at 43y 1m 21d.

W 4   FRY, Christena, b. 11 Aug 1804, d. 26 Jul 1877 at 72y 11m 15d.

RR 12   FRY, Daniel C. S., son of Noah & S. FRY, d. 2 May 1864 at 10y 2m 11d.

I 16   FRY, Elizabeth C., b. 24 Mar 1847, d. 18 Oct 1904.

E 6   FRY, Elizabeth, d. 15 Mar 1888 at 79y 11m 15d.

E 1   FRY, Elizabeth, d. 9 Oct 1890, at 60y 7m 8d.

R 14   FRY, Elizabeth, wife of Andrew FRY, d. 5 Jun 1873 at 80y 8m 4m.

X 5   FRY, Enos, b. 7 Aug 1842, d. 11 Sep 1852 at 10y 1m 1d.

DD 3   FRY, George W., b. 12 Apr 1838, d. 19 Feb 1872 at 33y 10m 7d.

U 2   FRY, Georgia, infant daughter of G. H. & C. FRY, d. 27 — 1897. [broken]

U 20   FRY, infant daughter of J. H. & S. E. FRY, d. 9 Jul 1871 at 5d.

U 19   FRY, infant son of Noah & S. FRY, d. 30 Oct 1857 at 8m 26d.

U 21   FRY, Ireneus F., son of Joseph H. & S. E. FRY, d. 28 Mar 1871 at 4y 6m 8d.

JJ 2   FRY, John A. N., son of George & Margaret FRY, b. 6 Aug 1865, d. 22 Mar 1867 at 1y 5m 16d.

E 5   FRY, John H., b. 25 Mar 1832, d. 27 May 1881 at 49y 2m 2d.

D 3   FRY, John P., d. 4 Oct 1888 at 55y 7m 22d.

W 3   FRY, John, b. 30 Dec 1791, d. 17 Jul 1877 at 85y 6m 17d.

S 19   FRY, Julius F., son of Noah & Susannah FRY, d. 12 Oct 1855.

S 22   FRY, Margaret A., b. 20 Nov 1813, d. 2 Aug 1899 at 85y 8m 12d.

DD 4   FRY, Martha E., wife of George W. FRY, b. 7 Apr 1842, d. 24 Sep 1874 at 32y 5m 17d.

Y 6   FRY, Mary C., wife of Jacob FRY, b. 19 Feb 1838, d. 18 Aug 1871 at 88y 5m 29d.

QQ 3   FRY, Mary Catherine, wife of John D. FRY, d. 24 Mar 1864 at 30y 11m 18d.

Pile   FRY, Mary E., daughter of Joseph & S. E. FRY, d. 12 Jul 1865 at 8m 12d.

List   FRY, Mary E., daughter of Joseph H. & S. E. FRY, d. 18 Mar 1864 at 8m 12d.

U 22   FRY, Mary, d. 18 Nov 1864 at 71y 2m.

W 10   FRY, Michael, b. 28 Feb 1785, d. 18 Jan 1817 at 61y 10m 20d.

W 2   FRY, Miss Lucinda, b. 1 Mar 1822, d. 1 Apr 1880.

V 3   FRY, Noah, b. 28 Nov 1828, d. 17 Aug 1903.

F 1   FRY, Peter, d. 26 Feb 1879 at 78y 4m 7d.

I 16   FRY, Philip, b. 3 Feb 1820, d. 25 Jun 1902.

KK 6   FRY, Philip, d. 11 Aug 1831 at 88 yrs.

FF 9   FRY, Philip, d. 2 Oct 1839 at 73y 2m.

EE 5   FRY, Polly, wife of John FRY, b. 20 May 1799, d. 24 Jun 1821 at 23y 26d.

EE 19   FRY, Robert W., d. 21 Mar 1890 at 7m 4d.

U 7   FRY, Samuel William, son of William & – FRY, d. 11 Dec 1833 at 2m 14d.

FF 10   FRY, Sarah Ann, daughter of William FRY, b. 30 Aug 1837, d. 9 Apr 1850 at 12y 7m 10d.

KK 26   FRY, Sarah C. E., wife of Daniel J. H. FRY, daughter of Samuel & Hannah COMPHER,
           b. 16 Sep 1840, d. 19 Sep 1867 at 27y 3d.

U 28   FRY, Sarah E., wife of David FRY, b. 23 Oct 1830, d. 13 Mar 1867.

EE 18   FRY, Sarah, d. 3 Dec 1866 at 61y 1m 28d.

V 3   FRY, Susannah, b. 4 Aug 1827, d. 27 Dec 1901.

H 4   FRY, Susannah, daughter of Michael & Susannah FRY, b. 6 May 1823, d. 15 Sep 1860.

W 9   FRY, Susannah, wife of Michael FRY, d. 26 Aug 1826 at 39 yrs.

List   FRY, Ulysses W., son of Joseph H. & S. E. FRY, d. 18 Mar 1867 at 5m 29d.

F 4   FRY, William, b. 30 Nov 1806, d. 11 May 1879.

List   FRYE, Addie Leslie, d. 12 Nov 1942 at 31y 5m 12d.

F 2   FRYE, Catherine A., daughter of Elizabeth FRYE, b. 8 Mar 1856, d. 7 May 1876.

List   FRYE, Charles Clayton, d. 16 Nov 1942 at 23y 9d.

KK 5   FRYE, Dorethy, wife of Philip FRYE, d. 31 Aug 1827 at 69y 2w 18d.

S 20   FRYE, infant son of Noah & Susannah FRYE, d. 11 Oct 1852.

BB 15   GOODHART, Sarah J. M., b. 13 Oct 1849, d. 26 Feb 1850.

BB 15   GOODHART, George E., d. 25 Jul 1854 at 15d.

N 9   GOODHART, Jacob, d. 12 Apr 1843 at 57y 9m 12d.

BB 15   GOODHART, John H. C., b. 8 Jul 1815, d. 29 Oct 1847.

BB 14   GOODHART, John H. Clay, son of Lawrence W. & Sophia GOODHART, d. 29 Oct 1847 at
         2y 2m 1d.

CC 7   GOODHART, Lydia E., daughter of J. W. & S. W. GOODHART, b. 30 Aug 1856,
         d. 20 Dec 1868.

CC 8   GOODHART, Mary S., daughter of J. W. & S. W. GOODHART, b. 24 Feb 1851,
         d. 13 Nov 1863.

N 8   GOODHART, Mary, wife of Jacob GOODHART, daughter of John FAWLEY, d. 4 Sep 1853 at
         65y 10m 11d.

CC 9   GOODHART, Sophia W., wife of J. W. GOODHART, b. 15 May 1817, d. 27 Feb 1871 at
         29y 8m 2d.

L 23   GRAHAM, George H., son of John & Mary GRAHAM, d. 4 Jan 1868 at 1y 10m 4d.

L 23   GRAHAM, Lydia E., daughter of John & Mary GRAHAM, d. 16 Nov 1864 at 3y 6m 20d.

L 23   GRAHAM, Mary C., daughter of John & Mary GRAHAM, d. 22 Sep 1857 at 1m 15d.

E 9   GREEN, L. Estella, b. 6 Apr 1873, d. 10 May 1926.

T 9   GRUBB, Alevia Catharine Charity, daughter of Benjamin & Rebecca GRUBB, d. 11 Jul 1843
         at 1y 8m 19d.

BB 3   GRUBB, Ebenezer, b. 1 Dec 1792, d. 1 Dec 1874 at 82 yrs.

T 10   GRUBB, Edward Curtis, son of Benjamin & Rebecca GRUBB, d. 24 Dec 1844 at 1y 10d.

U 13   GRUBB, Henry Clay, son of Benjamin J. & Rebecca GRUBB, d. 12 Jan 1841 at 4m 14d.

List   GRUBB, Jacob Curtis, son of E. L. & Cecilia GRUBB, b. 28 Jun 1821, d. 17 Oct 1824 at
         3y 3m 19d.

BB 1   GRUBB, John Ebenezer, son of E. L. & Cecilia GRUBB, b. 18 Jan 1855, d. 22 Aug 1855 at 7m 4d.

BB 2   GRUBB, Leah, wife of Ebenezer GRUBB, b. 13 Dec 1800, d. 14 Dec 1869 at 69y 1d.

T 11   GRUBB, Rebecca, wife of Benjamin J. GRUBB, d. 31 Jan 1849 at 40y 5m 19d.

K 8   HAMILTON, Caroline Amanda, wife of James W. HAMILTON, daughter of Gideon
         HOUSEHOLDER, b. 29 Nov 1823, d. 1 Mar 1853.

TT 12   HAMILTON, James W., b. 18 Dec 1820, d. 8 Oct 1863.

TT 13   HAMILTON, Lydia, daughter of James & Caroline HAMILTON, b. 5 Nov 1850,
    d. 12 Sep 1881.

Q 3   HAMILTON, Susan Elizabeth, daughter of James W. & Caroline A. HAMILTON,
    b. 14 Feb 1848, d. 2 Apr 1851.

Q 12   HART, Emma Jane, daughter of Joseph & Rachael A. HART, b. 14 Feb 1858, d. 30 Jun 1858 at
    4m 16d.

L 5   HAURER, Henrietta Warner, daughter of Daniel J. & Henrietta HAURER, d. 18 Aug 1842 at
    5y 8m 4d.

C 5   HAWES, Charles R., b. 9 Jun 1891, d. 1 Dec 1940.

BB 10   HECKMAN, Rachel, wife of Peter HECKMAN, d. 2 Sep 1816 at 32y 4m 3d.

G 1   HEFFNER, Elizabeth, wife of Frederick HEFFNER, d. 24 Jan 1874 at 78y 3m 16d.

F 8   HEFFNER, John, d. 6 Dec 1880 at 78y 3m 7d.

D 5   HEFFNER, Sarah, wife of John HEFFNER, d. 19 Nov 1895 at 87y 9m 4d.

U 29   HICKMAN, Benjamin J., b. 30 Sep 1848, d. 26 Jan 1871 at 22y 3m 26d.

U 24   HICKMAN, Caroline R., b. 28 Dec 1843, d. 15 Aug 1866.

J 8   HICKMAN, Catharine Amanda, daughter of Peter & Mary E. HICKMAN, b. 21 Nov 1847,
    d. 21 Apr 1856 at 8y 4m 27d.

H 6   HICKMAN, Catharine M., daughter of George & Eleanor HICKMAN, d. 11 Nov 1860 at
    2y 3m 12d.

H 14   HICKMAN, Catharine, d. 6 Jun 1869 at 54y 5m 5d.

R 9   HICKMAN, Catharine, wife of John HICKMAN, b. 20 Sep 1792, d. 1 Aug 1862 at
    69y 10m 12d.

U 26   HICKMAN, Elenora M., b. 7 Dec 1821, d. 10 Jun 1893.

U 25   HICKMAN, George, b. 14 Sep 1816, d. 27 Aug 1866.

RR 6   HICKMAN, John, b. 6 Dec 1816, d. 19 Nov 1863 at 46y 11m 3d.

V 7   HICKMAN, John, d. 13 Jan 1839 at 53y 1m 4d.

I 8   HICKMAN, Mary E., daughter of Peter & Mary C. HICKMAN, b. 21 Mar 1859,
    d. 11 Dec 1859.

H 12   HICKMAN, Mary E., wife of Peter HICKMAN, b. 25 Mar 1825, d. 9 Jan 1862.

V 9   HICKMAN, Mary, daughter of John & Catherine HICKMAN, b. 1 Mar 1813, d. 2 Jul 1841 at
    27y 1m 28d.

H 13   HICKMAN, Peter, b. 14 Aug 1818, d. 9 Sep 1863 at 45y 19d.

U 30   HICKMAN, Samuel P., d. 12 Mar 1921 at 75y 10d.

List   HICKMAN, Sarah S., d. 10 Feb 1834 at 31y 10m 28d.

RR 9   HICKMAN, William, b. 19 Oct 1814, d. 9 Jan 1864 at 49y 2m 20d.

V 1   HOUGH , Ola V., baby, d. 10 Jan 1877 at 1m 20d. [broken]

K 3   HOUGH, Charles K., b. 4 Jul 1823, d. 20 Sep 1853 at 30y 2m 16d.

K 14   HOUGH, Mary Ann, wife of John HOUGH, b. 26 May 1823, d. 28 Sep 1854.

K 2   HOUGH, Samuel Hampton, son of Charles K. & Ara O. HOUGH, b. 9 Mar 1849,
        d. 26 Apr 1854 at 5y 1m 17d.

BB 7   HOUSEHOLDER, Adam, b. 12 Feb 1808, d. 14 Sep 1882 at 74y 7m 2d.

L 8   HOUSEHOLDER, Caroline M., consort of Hamilton HOUSEHOLDER, b. 29 Sep 1827,
        d. 1 Sep 1849 at 21y 11m 2d.

BB 9   HOUSEHOLDER, Catharine, wife of Daniel HOUSEHOLDER, b. 12 Apr 1776,
        d. 21 Jun 1820.

I 6   HOUSEHOLDER, Catharine, wife of Jacob HOUSEHOLDER, b. 14 Aug 1817, d. 16 Aug 1859
        at 42y 2d.

BB 8   HOUSEHOLDER, Daniel, b. 15 Mar 1774, d. 17 Nov 1865 at 91y 8m 2d.

I 3   HOUSEHOLDER, George W., son of the late Gideon HOUSEHOLDER, b. 8 Dec 1841,
        d. 14 Jan 1859 at 17y 1m 6d.

Q 4   HOUSEHOLDER, Gideon, b. 5 Nov 1800, d. 15 Sep 1845 at 44y 10m 10d.

K 7   HOUSEHOLDER, Hamilton, b. 11 Nov 1826, d. 23 Feb 1853.

T 17   HOUSEHOLDER, Jacob, b. 27 Jun 1812, d. 2 Nov 1866.

Q 5   HOUSEHOLDER, Julia Ann, wife of Gideon HOUSEHOLDER, b. 8 Jun 1801, d. 7 Sep 1848 at
        47y 2m 29d.

BB 11   HOUSEHOLDER, Susanna Shafer, wife of Adam HOUSEHOLDER, d. 2 Sep 1819 at 61 yrs.

T 18   HOUSEHOLDER, Valeria G., b. 26 Dec 1856, d. 3 Nov 1866.

T 19   HOUSEHOLDER, Virginia C., b. 23 Jan 1844, d. 27 Nov 1866.

KK 15   HOUSHOLTER, Adam, d. 27 Sep 1804 at 55 yrs.

KK 14   HOUSHOLTER, Catharine, wife of Adam HOUSHOLTER, d. 10 Sep 1794 at 44 yrs.

KK 16   HUF, Philip, d. 9 Mar 1796 at 33y 3m.

EE 7   HUNT, Jacob, 1806 [broken fieldstone]

NN 16   HUNTER, Amanda C., wife of George P. HUNTER, b. 22 Jan 1827, d. 8 Oct 1895 at
        68y 9m 16d.

NN 15   HUNTER, George P., b. 7 Sep 1831, d. 4 Apr 1907 at 75y 6m 27d.

NN 9   HUNTER, Ida C., daughter of M. L. & Margaret HUNTER, d. 6 Feb 1866 at 1y 3m 12d.

L 21   HUNTER, infant daughter of Michael & Marguretta HUNTER, b. & d. 1 Sep 1877.

NN 8   HUNTER, Margaret, wife of Michael L. HUNTER, b. 19 Aug 1838, d. 17 Sep 1865 at 27y 29d.

NN 14   HUNTER, Michael L., b. 12 Jul 1834, d. 3 Jun 1876 at 41y 10m 12d.

TT 17   HUNTER, Sevila, wife of William HUNTER, b. 13 Jul 1795, d. 25 Feb 1862 at 66y 7m 12d.

NN 10   HUNTER, Walter, son of M. L. & R. H. HUNTER, b. 19 Jun 1873, d. 7 Oct 1873.

TT 14   HUNTER, William, b. 11 Mar 1798, d. 21 Jul 1863 at 65y 4m 9d.

Pile   I. G. S. 1785.

LL 5   JACOBS , Sarah, wife of Bynard JACOBS, b. 25 Mar 1813, d. 19 Apr 1881 at 68y 24d.

List   JACOBS, Chester R., son of John & Mary JACOBS, d. 14 Sep 1892 at 8m.

L 17   JACOBS, Eliza Elinor, daughter of William H. & Catharine JACOBS, d. 5 Jul 1842 at
         5y 1m 25d.

LL 8   JACOBS, James W., d. 15 Jan 1902 at 59y 9m 7d.

Pile   JACOBS, John S., d. 23 Dec 1864 at 37 yrs.

DD 7   JACOBS, Nellie B., daughter of John & Mary JACOBS, d. 6 Sep 1892 at 8y 5m 22d.

L 16   JACOBS, Sarah Catharine Wise, daughter of William H. & Catharine JACOBS,
         d. 14 Mar 1843 at 1y 11m 12d.

JJ 3   JACOBS, Sarah F. E., daughter of James W. & Catharine H. JACOBS, d. 4 Aug 1867 at
         5m 14d.

I 7   JACOBS, Wm. H., d. 7 Sep 1859 at 62 yrs.

K 18   JOHNSON, Lydia Jane, wife of Henry A. JOHNSON, b. 5 Jan 1834, d. 15 Feb 1860.

NN 4   JOUER, John, b. 19 Feb 1788, d. 19 Feb 1826.

UU 14   KABRICK, Peter J., b. 28 Apr 1831, d. 21 Sep 1862.

U 4   KALB, Charles K., son of S. A. & L. A. KALB, d. 30 Aug 1874 at 3y 11m.

S 18   KALB, infant daughter of John G. R. & Ellen M. KALB, b. 25 Mar 1863.

List   KALB, Margarett Susan, daughter of John G. R. & Ellen M. KALB, d. 6 Apr 1861 at 11y 9d.

U 12   KERN, Aaron J., b. 27 Mar 1819, d. 3 Apr 1819 at 17d.

U 11   KERN, Benjamin, d. 10 Mar 1833 at 3y 11m 10d.

H 3   KERN, Elizabeth, b. 12 Nov 1781, d. 6 Dec 1861 at 80y 25d.

H 2   KERN, Jacob, b. 15 Aug 1776, d. 29 Aug 1860 at 84y 24d.

PP 3   KERN, Margaret, d. 24 Mar 1864 at 58y 10m 19d.

H 1   KERN, William, d. 19 Jul 1885 at 77y 3m 3d.

List   LANN, James W., 12 Nov 1932 at 68 yrs.

K 23   LEE, Julia Ettie, b. 3 Apr 1846, d. 14 Oct 1911.

W 20   LEWIS, Anna J., wife of John H. LEWIS, d. 7 Jan 1884 at 25y 6m 4d.

C 1   LEWIS, Caroline E., b. 25 Jul 1830, d. 14 May 1898.

K 20   LEWIS, Charles M., b. 20 May 1840, d. 22 Oct 1863 at 23y 5m 2d.

K 19   LEWIS, infant of Charles M. & Elizabeth LEWIS.

W 21   LEWIS, John H., b. 3 May 1854, d. 17 Nov 1935.

L 20   LEWIS, Laura F., daughter of Robert A. & Caroline M. LEWIS, b. 30 Nov 1851, d. 16 Jun 1876.

W 19   LEWIS, Mary C. E., daughter of Robt. & Caroline LEWIS, d. 19 May 1878 at 28y 8m 24d.

RR 13   LEWIS, Mitta M. F., daughter of Robert & Caroline A. LEWIS, b. 6 May 1863, d. 18 Oct 1864
            at 1y 5m.

C 1   LEWIS, Robert S., b. 31 Jul 1825, d. 27 Aug 1905.

J 10   LUCKETT, Charles W. [sunken]

L 11   LUCKETT, Luther C., b. 9 Sep 1818, d. 31 May 1844 at 25y 8m 22d.

J 1   LUCKETT, Mary B., daughter of Samuel C. & Mary B. LUCKETT, b. 26 Nov 1846,
            d. 16 Mar 1890.

K 10   LUCKETT, Mary B., wife of Samuel C. LUCKETT, b. 14 May 1809, d. 9 Oct 1853.

I 1   LUCKETT, Samuel C., b. 6 Nov 1807, d. 7 Aug 1893 at 85y 9m 1d.

QQ 6   LUCKETT, Samuel C., youngest son of Samuel C. & Mary B. LUCKETT, d. 28 Feb 1867 at
            15 yrs.

QQ 5   LUCKETT, Virginia C., eldest daughter of Samuel C. & Mary B. LUCKETT, d. 23 Aug 1864
            at 25 yrs.

LL 4   LYNN, Elizabeth, b. 11 Oct 1805, d. 8 Mar 1867 at 61y 4m 27d.

W 18   LYNN, Lydia Jane, b. 14 Apr 1845, d. 15 Mar 1905.

LL 3   LYNN, Nicholas, b. 21 Nov 1804, d. 18 Jul 1866 at 61y 7m 27d.

GG 3   MAN, Leanah, wife of John MAN, daughter of Philip EVERHART, b. 28 Jan 1806,
            d. 31 Dec 1824 at 18y 11m 3d.

L 2   MANN, Anna Maria, wife of John MANN, b. 4 May 1775, d. 3 May 1859 at 83y 11m 30d.

List   MANN, Catharine, infant daughter of William & Margaret MANN, d. 1851.

H 10	MANN, Charity, daughter of Edward & Flora MORRISON, b. 23 Oct 1833, d. 24 Sep 1860 at 26y 11m 1d.

PP 5	MANN, Elizabeth, wife of Joseph MANN, b. 28 Nov 1807, d. 5 Apr 1879.

I 2	MANN, George William, b. 24 Jul 1819, d. 13 Apr 1858 at 38y 8m 20d.

G 7	MANN, Ida A., daughter of George & Leanna MANN, d. 15 May 1862 at 9y 22d.

W 1	MANN, infant son of J. W. & E. S. MANN, d. 23 Feb 1902.

K 16	MANN, Jacob F., son of Joseph & Elizabeth MANN, b. 25 Nov 1839, d. 20 Jun 1858 at 18y 6m 25d.

N 12	MANN, Joannah Elizabeth, daughter of Joseph & Elizabeth MANN, b. 27 Sep 1836, d. 2 Oct 1845.

L 4	MANN, John, d. 22 May 1851 at 83y 3m 18d.

PP 6	MANN, Joseph, b. 12 Oct 1804, d. 12 Jul 1864 at 59y 9m.

List	MANN, Lewis W., son of Joseph & Elizabeth MANN, b. 27 Jul 1830, d. 23 Aug 1867 at 37 yrs.

GG 4	MANN, Louisa Ann, daughter of John & Anna Mary MANN, d. 25 Jun 1817 at 5y 3m 13d.

List	MANN, Martin L., son of John & Charity MANN, b. 21 Sep 1860, d. 17 Mar 1861.

List	MANN, Mary C., daughter of John & Charity MANN, 25 Sep 1859, d. 19 Jul 1860.

SS 1	MANN, Mary E, daughter of Jacob & Ann MANN, b. 6 Oct 1851, d. 17 Jun 1863 at 11y 8m 11d.

BB 19	MANN, Mary E., daughter of C. & J. MANN, d. 27 Jan 1874 at 2m 26d.

P 14	MANN, Peter Silas, son of John & Sarah MANN, b. 1 Nov 1826, d. 11 Sep 1850.

CC 13	MANN, Rosetta May, d. 2 Mar 1891 at 10m 7d.

G 6	MANN, Sarah, wife of John MANN, b. 5 Apr 1810, d. 10 Mar 1877.

SS 1	MANN, Virginia E., daughter of Jacob & Ann MANN, b. 30 Jan 1854, d. 30 Jun 1863 at 9y 5m.

K 17	MARCHE, Anna L., d. 26 Jun 1867 at 1y 7d.

LL 6	McDONOUGH, Bettie, daughter of L. H. & E. A. McDONOUGH, b. 17 Sep 1866, d. 15 Aug 1868.

LL 6	McDONOUGH, Willie, son of L. H. & E. A. McDONOUGH, b. 4 Aug 1864, d. 9 May 1870.

Y 8	MILES, Annie I., wife of John W. MILES, b. 4 Jul 1851, d. 8 Feb 1876 at 24y 7m 4d.

EE 4	MILLER, Michael, d. Sep 1806 at 35y a few days.

K 15	MILLER, Nancy, d. 30 Dec 1851 at 73 yrs.

GG 5	MOORE, Elenor I., daughter of John & Mary E. MOORE, d. 22 Jan 1825 at 11m 19d.

W 11	MORGAN, Eliza, wife of Philip MORGAN, b. 15 Dec 1807, d. 8 Sep 1829.

W 11   MORGAN, Mary M., b. 1826, d. 1829.

J 12   MORRISON, Edward, b. 22 Jun 1785, d. 13 Apr 1858 at 72y 9m 21d.

EE 11   MORRISON, George Henry Clay, son of Archibald & Mary M. MORRISON, d. 15 Sep 1854
           at 1y 2m 28d.

EE 10   MORRISON, Hannah Ann, daughter of Archibald & Rachel MORRISON, d. 16 Jul 1851
           at 14d.

EE 13   MORRISON, Rachel, wife of Archibald MORRISON, b. 8 Aug 1818, d. 24 Jan 1852 at
           33y 5m 16d.

EE 12   MORRISON, Sophia E., daughter of Archibald & Rachel MORRISON, d. 15 Sep 1854 at
           11y 5m 1d.

TT 11   MYERS, Peter C., b. 30 Sep 1813, d. 23 Aug 1863 at 49y 10m 23d.

K 5   MYERS, Sarah Jane, daughter of William & Catherine MYERS, b. 28 Feb 1851,
           d. 30 Sep 1854 at 3y 7m 2d.

J 16   OREM, Mary P., wife of Nathanel OREM, d. 28 Nov 1882 at 32y 1 m 4d.

G 3   ORME, Eliza A., wife of Robert S. ORME, b. 22 Feb 1812, d. 1 Jan 1876 at 63y 10m 9d.

D 2   ORME, Robert S., son of Archibald & Etta ORME, d. 21 Jan 1884 at 74y 4m 15d.

V 8   ORRISON, James, son of William D. & Elizabeth ORRISON, b. 15 Oct 1842, d. 14 Oct 1845
           at 3 yrs.

LL 7   PARSON, Hector, infant of T. M. & S. J. PARSON, b. 28 Jan 1870, d. 10 Jul 1870 at
           5m 12d. [broken]

AA 4   POTTERFIELD, Catharine, consort of Samuel POTTERFIELD, b. 25 Dec 1806, d. 16 Aug 1846
           at 39y 7m 21d.

I 5   POTTERFIELD, Elizabeth, relict of Jacob POTTERFIELD , d. 31 July 1859 at 79y 4m 16d.
           [broken]

RR 7   POTTERFIELD, Samuel, b. 1 Mar 1799, d. 17 Nov 1863 at 64y 8m 16d.

K 17   REED, Charles A., d. Feb 1864 at 14 yrs.

List   RICHARDS, Samuel D., b. 18 Jul 1823, d. 12 Sep 1836.

Pile   RICHARDSON, Virginia C., daughter of Rev. X. J. RICHARDSON, d. 28 Jun 1868 at 12y
           9m 17d.

S 21   RICHARSON, H. M. M., infant son of Rev. X. J. & M. I. RICHARDSON, d. 4 Jan 1865 at 16d.

BB 6   RICKARD, Catharine, wife of George RICKARD, d. 7 Sep 1823 at 28y 23d.

BB 5   RICKERT, Amila, daughter of George RICKERT, d. 25 Jul 1816 at 7m 3w 4d. [broken]

Pile   ROFF, Johannes, d. 1794 at 43y 2m 3w. [German inscription]

FF 11   ROLER, Conrad, b. 7 Feb 1786, d. 11 Aug 1852 at 66y 6m 7d.

EE 1   ROLLER, Christian, son of Conrad ROLLER, d. 18 Jun 1797 at 2y 7m.

CC 1   ROLLER, Conrad, d. 8 Oct 1824 at 72y 7m 1w 5d.

CC 2   ROLLER, Elizabeth, d. 22 Feb 1845 at 83y 2m 11d.

DD 6   ROLLER, Frederick, b. 17 Jan 1799, d. 20 Jan 1875 at 85y 3d.

Q 7   ROLLER, John, b. 11 Dec 1781, d. 30 May 1843 at 61y 5m 19d.

OO 4   ROLLER, John, d. 26 Sep 1802 at 71y 10m 5d.

DD 5   ROLLER, Rachel, b. 1 Nov 1799, d. 25 Mar 1872 at 72y 4m 21d.

Pile   ROLLER, Rosena, wife of John ROLLER, d. 30 Feb 1794 at 69y 3m.

EE 2   ROLLER, Samuel, son of Conrad ROLLER, d. 8 Oct 1805 at 1yr.

W 14   ROPP, Rachel, wife of Samuel ROPP, b. 2 Apr 1821, d. 4 Nov 1848 at 27y 7m 2d.

Q 2   ROPP, William M., son of Samuel & Rachel ROPP, b. 29 Aug 1845, d. 19 Aug 1846.

J 7   RUSE, Annie E., wife of Edward S. RUSE, and only daughter of the late George SLATER,
            b. 20 Feb 1835, d. 20 Dec 1855 at 20y 10m.

NN 2   RUSE, Catharine, d. 15 Aug 1802 at 35 yrs.

NN 1   RUSE, Christian, d. 20 Sep 1821 at 75 yrs. [illegible]

NN 3   RUSE, Elizabeth, d. 1807 at –y 8m 3w. [illegible]

PP 10   RUSE, Henry, d. 2 Feb 1865 at 71y 4m 8d.

NN 11   RUSE, Mary A., daughter of Henry & Sarah RUSE, d. 16 Mar 1865 at 28y 4m 26d.

PP 8   RUSE, Michael, d. 26 Oct 1864 at 78y 8m 8d. [broken]

PP 9   RUSE, Sallie, wife of Henry RUSE, d. 19 Nov 1894 at 91y 10m 6d.

V 10   RUST, Catherine H., daughter of James W. & Margaret RUST, b. 13 Oct 1845, d. 23 Jan 1848
            at 2y 3m 10d.

R 11   RUST, James W., b. 11 Dec 1819, d. 28 Feb 1866 at 46y 2m 12d.

H 11   RUST, Margaret A., wife of James W. RUST, d. 4 Dec 1861 at 38y 1m 29d.

T 1   SACKMAN, Sarah, d. 10 Feb 1831 at 31y 10m 23d.

Pile   SCHAEFFER, Elizabeth, d. 9 Jan 1897 at 90y 10m 1d.

Q 16   SCHAEFFER, Jacob, d. 3 Dec 1873 at 69y 7m.

Q 18   SCHAEFFER, Malinda, daughter of Jacob SCHAEFFER, d. 2 Feb 1879 at 70y 11m 8d.

Q 17   SCHAFFER, Henry, d. 4 Nov 1876 at 76yrs.

S 7   SCHAFFER, Mary Elizabeth, b. 13 Apr 1835 at 64y 6m 8d.

GG 2   SCHMIDT, Jacob, d. 21 Feb 1796. [German inscription]

Pile   SCHMIT, H. L. John, d. 21 Oct 1793.

FF 7   SCHWANK, Catharine, b. 10 Sep 1776, d. 11 Dec 1850 at 74y 3m 1d.

List   SHAEFER, Michael, d. 5 Mar 1839 at 25y 15d.

RR 14   SHAFER, Harry, infant son of John H. & Emma C. SHAFER, d. 22 Jan 1864.

P 8   SHAFER, John, d. 10 Mar 1838 at 72 yrs.

S 6   SHAFFER, Christena, d. 23 Apr 1833 at 22y 3m 12d.

S 8   SHAFFER, Henry, d. 1 Jan 1832 at 38y 1m 23d.

P 9   SHAFFER, John William, son of Joseph B. & Susan SHAFFER, b. 11 Oct 1852, d. 16 Apr 1853
           at 6m 2d.

P 11   SHAFFER, John, b. 1 Mar 1807, d. 10 Sep 1843 at 36y 3m 9d.

BB 12   SHAFFER, John, d. 13 Jan 1828 at 27y 10m 16d.

S 5   SHAFFER, Lucinda, d. 1 Jan 1833 at 18y 10m 19d.

P 10   SHAFFER, Mary, d. 22 Apr 1842 at 75 yrs.

T 2   SHAFFER, Michael, d. 5 Mar 1830 at 25y 13d.

List   SHAFFER, Michael, Sr., d. 30 Jan 1829 at 59y 7m 1d.

II 18   SHEWMAKER, Leah, daughter of Simon & Catharine SHEWMAKER, b. 26 Dec 1830,
           d. 16 Aug 1832.

II 19   SHUMAKER, Catharine, wife of Simon SHUMAKER, b. 18 Sep 1790, d. 23 Feb 1857 at
           66y 5m 5d.

E 4   SHUMAKER, Catherine, b. 16 Jan 1807, d. 3 Jan 1894 at 86y 11m 17d.

E 3   SHUMAKER, John, b. 6 Nov 1796, d. 14 May 1881 at 84y 6m 8d.

EE 8   SHUMAKER, Jonathan, b. 2 Feb 1816, 14 Sep 1863 at 47y 6m 14d.

E 8   SHUMAKER, Margaret, b. 16 Aug 1824, d. 11 May 1882.

F 6   SHUMAKER, Mary, d. 1 Jun 1879 at 68y 3m 11d.

EE 9   SHUMAKER, Simon, b. 1 Oct 1784, d. 10 Apr 1857 at 72y 6m 9d.

UU 9   SIMONS, Henry M., son of Edward & Mary A. SIMONS, d. 10 Aug 1863 at 19y 1m 25d.

UU 10   SIMONS, William E. F. J., son of Edward & Mary Ann SIMONS, b. 30 Oct 1855,
           d. 7 Mar 1859 at 3y 4m 8d.

K 1   SLATER, Ann Eliza, wife of Samuel W. SLATER, daughter of Samuel & Mary
               STOUTSENBERGER, b. 26 Jul 1836, d. 3 Mar 1857.

K 4   SLATER, Barbary, wife of Samuel SLATER, b. 1 Aug 1808, d. 20 Aug 1854 at 46y 19d.

J 2   SLATER, Catherine, consort of Jacob SLATER, b. 1 Jan 1769, d. 13 Apr 1857.

S 16   SLATER, Catherine, infant child of William & Margaret SLATER, d. 12 Feb 1835.

FF 2   SLATER, Catherine, wife of John SLATER, d. 6 Sep 1807 at 35yrs.

U 27   SLATER, George, d. 17 Nov 1866 at 71y 1m 18d.

X 3   SLATER, Jacob, d. 29 Oct 1898 at 59y 1m 14d.

FF 1   SLATER, John, d. 15 Jan 1824 at 60y 2m 22d.

S 17   SLATER, Mary, daughter of William & Margaret SLATER, d. 5 Dec 184– [broken] at 6yrs.

X 2   SLATER, Michael, son of John SLATER, d. 8 Feb 1826 at 24y 3m 23d.

U 31   SLATER, Sarah, wife of George SLATER, d. 5 Sep 1878 at 79y 20d.

AA 8   SMITH, Henry T., son of Job & Lydia SMITH, b. 23 Feb 1851, d. 18 Aug 1871 at 20y 5m 25d.

OO 5   SMITH, Jacob, 13 Apr 1805 at 61y 11m.

DD 2   SMITH, John A., b. 1 Mar 1851, d. 10 Aug 1870 at 19y 5m 9d.

L 13   SMITH, Mary, b. 29 Jul 1799, d. 25 Aug 1851.

CC 5   SMITH, Susannah, wife of T. SMITH, d. 7 Mar 1826 at 82y 4m 1d.

EE 3   SMITH, William, d. 26 Mar 1808 at 22y 9m.

K 13   SNOOTS, John, b. 21 Oct 1838, d. 22 Sep 1854 at 15y 10m 29d.

M 5   SNOOTS, Susan R., daughter of John & Anna J. SNOOTS, b. 22 Sep 1853, d. 9 Nov 1854 at
               1y 1m 18d.

M 6   SPEAKS, Margaret C. A., daughter of Richard & Mary E. SPEAKS, b. 6 Sep 1855,
               d. 27 Nov 1855 at 2m 21d.

Z 1   SPEAKS, Sytha Ann Vyletter, daughter of Charles C. & Sarah Ann SPEAKS, b. 17 Feb 1851,
               d. 1 Mar 1851 at 12d.

List   SPINKS, Cornell F., d. 21 Apr 1941 at 55y 7d.

List   SPINKS, Elizabeth V., d. 2 Jul 1935 at 80y 4m 18d.

G 9   SPINKS, James, Lizzie, Amie, Mamie, Mary. [no dates]

BB 17   SPRING, Casper, b. 16 Apr 1788, d. 4 Jan 1868 at 79y 8m 19d.

F 7   SPRING, Charlott, d. 26 May 1880 at 81 yrs.

BB 18   SPRING, Elizabeth, wife of Casper SPRING, d. 6 Sep 1883 at 91y 11m 3d.

RR 10   SPRING, George F., d. 13 Feb 1864 at 18y 5m 12d.

PP 7   SPRING, John, d. Oct 1865 at 65 yrs.

TT 16   SPRING, Lillie C., daughter of Charles W. & Laura J. SPRING, d. 14 May 1875 at 5m 1d.

P 12   SPRING, Lydia Ann, consort of Elias SPRING, b. 22 Dec 1830, d. 28 Dec 1847 at 17y 6d.

KK 22   STATLER, John, d. 30 Jun 1856 at 97 yrs.

KK 21   STATLER, Priscilla, d. 28 Feb 1852 at 85 yrs.

RR 2   STONE, Edgar H., b. 4 Dec 1852, d. 14 Jan 1877 at 24y 1m 10d.

RR 3   STONE, Eleanor W., daughter of Samuel & Elizabeth STONE, d. 26 Jun 1865 at 18y 3m 26d.

List   STONE, Michael, son of Frederick STONE, b. 2 May 1762, d. 28 Feb 1835.

RR 5   STONE, Samuel F., son of Samuel & Elizabeth STONE, b. 30 Sep 1844, d. 30 Oct 1863 at 19y 1m.

RR 1   STONE, Samuel S., d. 13 Mar 1880 at 69y 18d.

RR 4   STONE, Thomas M., son of Samuel & Elizabeth STONE, d. 19 Apr 1865 at 24y 9m 9d.

FF 3   STONBEBURNER, Adam, d. 11 Jan 1826 at 31y 4m 21d.

W 8   STONEBURNER, Anna Mary, d. 1 Nov 1844 at 75 yrs.

X 13   STONEBURNER, Catharine, b. 5 Sep 1801, d. 16 Sep 1879 at 79y 11d.

W 7   STONEBURNER, Daniel, b. 15 Jun 1767, d. 14 Oct 1826 at 59y 3m 29d.

X 9   STONEBURNER, Daniel, b. 5 Aug 1796, d. 12 Apr 1869.

List   STONEBURNER, George, d. 11 Jan 1826 at 31y 4m 21d.

L 18   STONEBURNER, infant son of J. C. & C. E. STONEBURNER, d. 3 Dec 1855.

GG 6   STONEBURNER, John Leonitus, d. 18 Oct 1825 at 2y 1m.

OO 2   STONEBURNER, Juliana, wife of Frederick STONEBURNER, b. 20 Mar 1762, d. 28 Feb 1799 at 36y 11m.

M 4   STONEBURNER, Laura Jane, daughter of Peter & Catherine STONEBURNER, d. 22 Sep 1851 at 2y 8d.

X 12   STONEBURNER, Sarah, b. May 1808, d. 1 Jun 1875 at 67 yrs.

P 4   STOUTSENBERGER, John, b. 2 Apr 1762, d. 31 Mar 1837 at 74y 11m 29d.

P 3   STOUTSENBERGER, Maria M., relict of John STOUTSENBERGER, d. 9 Oct 1847 at 85y 5m 23d.

KK 18   STOUTSENBERGER, Mary, wife of Samuel STOUTSENBERGER, b. 11 May 1826, d. 8 Sep 1854 at 28yrs.

KK 20   STOUTSENBERGER, Mary, consort of Samuel STOUTSENBERGER, b. 11 Apr 1801,
         d. 11 Jun 1842 at 41y 2m.

KK 19   STOUTSENBERGER, Samuel, b. 13 Dec 1801, d. 13 Mar 1847 at 45y 3m.

C 2   STREAM, Jacob H., d. 27 Sep 1904, at 72y 1m 17d.

U 9   STUCK, Charles A., son of F. F. & Jane STUCK, b. 28 Aug 1825, d. 30 Sep 1829.

N 19   STUCK, Elizabeth, b. 13 Mar 1773, d. 7 Aug 1850 at 77y 4m 24d.

U 8   STUCK, Joseph Henry, son of F. F. & Jane STUCK, b. 15 Oct 1823, d. 2 Oct 1841.

M 1   STUCK, Mary M., d. 18 Jul 1851 at 41y 21d.

N 18   STUCK, Peter, b. 20 Sep 1766, d. 4 May 1846 at 79y 7m 14d.

U 10   STUCK, Peter, son of F. F. & Jane STUCK, b. 4 Sep 1827, d. 14 Oct 1830.

Y 5   SWANK, Alcinda, b. 15 Oct 1822, d. 28 Mar 1871 at 48y 5m 12d.

EE 14   SWANK, Mary, wife of Philip SWANK, b. 23 Sep 1786, d. 15 May 1839.

CC 11   SWANK, Peter, son of Philip & Mary SWANK, b. 6 Jan 1826, d. 27 May 1847.

KK 23   SWANK, Philip, b. 10 Jan 1782, d. 8 Aug 1854 at 72y 6m 29d.

Y 9   TALTON, George W., d. 13 Apr 1911 at 42y 1m.

L 3   TRITAPOE, John H., son of Charles & L. A. TRITAPOE, b. 2 Apr 1866, d. 4 Aug 1867 at
         1y 4m 2d.

CC 14   TRITAPOE, Laura Millannette, daughter of Samuel & Sarah F. TRITAPOE, b. 20 Feb 1870,
         d. 9 Jun 1875 at 5y 3m 18d.

R 15   TRITAPOE, Michael, d. 4 Jul 1873 at 75y 2m 8d.

OO 1   VCKENS, Isack L. - 1770. [fieldstone]

T 13   VICKERS, Catharine, wife of William VICKERS, b. 24 Oct 1811, d. 14 Aug 1847 at
         35y 9m 21d.

L 27   VICKERS, Eunice A., daughter of Richard & J. T. VICKERS, b. 14 Nov 1879, d. 20 Dec 1879.

AA 5   VICKERS, Isabel F., daughter of William & Sarah VICKERS, d. 3 Aug 1852 at 4y 2d.

CC 18   VICKERS, John T., b. 12 Jan 1845, d. 29 Mar 1910.

L 19   VICKERS, Josephine L., d. 10 May 1856, 1y 11m 22d.

U 14   VICKERS, Mary Amanda, daughter of William & Catherine VICKERS, b. 11 Nov 1832,
         d. 30 Nov 1833.

CC 16   VICKERS, Rachel A. C., wife of John T. VICKERS, b. 9 Sep 1846, d. 22 Feb 1896 [stone lists
         children: Allice, John G. , Thomas H., Ellen C., Charles, Eunice L., Edward F.,
         James H., Mary G., Susannah, Samuel, and William].

EE 20   VICKERS, Samuel, son of J. T. & Rachel VICKERS, b. 10 Dec 1889, d. 10 Apr 1891 at 1y 4m.

G 5   VINCEL, Catharine, wife of George VINCEL, d. 27 Nov 1894 at 86y 11d.

TT 15   VINCEL, Delilah, wife of Luther H. VINCEL, b. 20 Dec 1838, d. 30 Oct 1863 at 24 yrs.

N 20   VINCEL, George T., d. 5 Sep 1856 at 34y 6m.

G 4   VINCEL, George, d. 21 Oct 1876 at 71y 4m.

W 15   VINCEL, John, son of John VINCEL, Sr., b. 3 Jan 1792, d. 27 Dec 1826.

J 14   VINCEL, Margaret Jane, daughter of Solomon & Louisa VINCEL, b. 15 Apr 1845,
           d. 13 Jun 1858.

R 3   VINCEL, Mary C., daughter of Philip & Louisa VINCEL, b. 3 Oct 1828, d. 28 Nov 1847 at
           19y 1m 25d.

S 9   VINCEL, Mary M., b. 26 Jul 1766, d. 17 Sep 1846 at 80y 1m 21d.

N 7   VINCEL, Solomon, b. 27 Jul 1808, d. 29 Oct 1854 at 46y 3m 2d.

BB 20   VINCIL, Ginettie, b. 27 Aug 1848, d. 8 Mar 1871 at 22y 6m 11d.

V 4   VINSEL, Adam, son of John A. VINSEL, b. 17 Feb 1790, d. 23 Aug 1827 at 36y 4m 25d.

S 10   VINSEL, John, Sr., b. 10 Jan 1764, d. 27 Mar 1835 at 71 yrs.

List   VIRTS, Anna E., b. 7 Jul 1851, d. 24 Oct 1906.

FF 5   VIRTS, Elizabeth, wife of Michael VIRTS, b. 19 Jun 1816, d. 5 Oct 1857 at 41y 3m 16d.

H 7   VIRTS, Henry, 1822 - 1861.

Y 7   VIRTS, John A., b. 25 May 1806, d. 9 Nov 1874 at 68y 5m 14d.

N 13   VIRTS, Leah, wife of Peter VIRTS, b. 15 May 1812, d. 14 Sep 1849 at 36y 4m.

PP 1   VIRTS, Lucy Ann, daughter of Peter & Leah VIRTS, b. 17 May 1838, d. 28 Aug 1864 at
           26y 3m 11d.

List   VIRTS, Mary Ann, wife of Peter VIRTS, b. 5 Nov –, d. – Feb –.

FF 6   VIRTS, Michael, b. 2 Jun 1797, d. 4 Sep 1851 at 54y 2m 2d.

Q 8   VIRTS, Phebe, wife of W. VIRTS, d. 29 Apr 1845 at 57 yrs.

H 7   VIRTS, Virginia, 1829 - 1902.

PP 4   VIRTS, William H., son of Peter & Leah VIRTS, b. 28 Dec 1842, d. 8 Aug 1867.

BB 16   VIRTS, William, b. 4 Dec 1771, d. 9 Dec 1853 at 82y 5d.

L 24   VIRTS, Willie, infant son of William H. & Marietta VIRTS, d. 17 Apr 1872 at 9d.

OO 6   VIRTZ, Barbary E., d. 1790 at 57 yrs.

KK 2   VIRTZS, Christine, wife of Peter VIRTZS, d. 20 Jun 1813 at 76y 5m 3w 2d.

KK 1   VIRTZS, Peter, son of John VIRTZS, d. 23 Apr 1812 at 35y 2m 1w 2d.

CC 17   WADE, Ellenor, d. 5 Oct 1900 at 83yrs.

II 8   WALMAN, Sara, daughter of John WALMAN, d. 10 Mar 1816 at 9m 2w.

X 8   WALTMAN, Col. Enanuel, b. 6 Dec 1797, d. 2 Dec 1866 at 68y 11m 26d.

II 7   WALTMAN, Emanuel, son of Jacob WALTMAN, Sr., d. 24 Jan 1821 at 15y 9m.

KK 10   WALTMAN, Georg Freiedrich Emanuel, d. 1800 at 38y 11m. [German inscription]

KK 11   WALTMAN, Imanuel, d. 13 Feb 1784 at 69 yrs.

Pile   WALTMAN, Jacob, b. 6 Nov 1793, d. 21 Apr 1865 at 71y 5m 15d.

II 9   WALTMAN, Jacob, Sr., d. 8 Oct 1823 at 78 yrs.

II 6   WALTMAN, Jacob; Margaret, his wife; Elizabeth, his second wife; Elias, his son died
           12 May 1827 at 24 yrs. [Elias' death date]

List   WALTMAN, John.

X 7   WALTMAN, Joseph, b. 11 Feb 1800, d. 21 Jun 1870.

II 12   WALTMAN, Margaret H., wife of Jacob WALTMAN, Sr., d. 15 Jan 1809 at 65 yrs.

KK 13   WALTMAN, Margaret, daughter of Jacob WALTMAN, d. Jan 1789 at 17y 6m 8d.

KK 12   WALTMAN, Margaret, wife of Imanuel, d. 13 Oct 1786 at 57yrs.

II 11   WALTMAN, Margaret, wife of Jacob WALTMAN, d. 30 Jan 1807 at 30y 11m 10d.

List   WALTMAN, Martha, wife of W. WALTMAN, 13 Oct 1806. [no other date]

KK 10   WALTMAN, William, son of John WALTMAN, d. 23 May 1813.

TT 10   WEBSTER, Alice S., daughter of J. M. & A. E. DOWNEY, 1 Aug 1863 at 22 yrs.

K 21   WENNER, Alberta Alder, daughter of Jonathan & Mary C. WENNER, d. 25 Jun 1871
           at 5m 9d.

K 21   WENNER, Jonathan A., d. 13 Oct 1882 at 41y 5m.

Q 14   WENNER, Lydia Jane, daughter of J. W. & L. WENNER, d. 31 Mar 1869 at 21y 5m 5d.

K 21   WENNER, Mary C., wife of Jonathan A. WENNER, b. 27 Sep 1841, d. 16 Aug 1916.

N 17   WENNER, Sarah, relict of John WENNER, d. 16 May 1850 at 49y 8m 4d.

R 12   WENNER, William C., son of J. W. & L. WENNER, d. 5 Oct 1870 at 1y 2m 22d.

F 5   WERKING, George, b. 18 Feb 1822, d. 19 May 1879 at 52y 8m 1d.

QQ 7   WHITE, Crawford K., d. 3 Dec 1865 at 38 yrs.

K 9   WHITE, Elizabeth, daughter of William & Maria WHITE, b. 22 Oct 1821, d. 28 Aug 1854 at
           29y 10m 6d.

L 10   WHITE, Rebecca, d. 14 May 1850 at 23 yrs.

AA 6   WHITEHOUSE, Mary J., b. 27 Feb 1837, d. 1 Jul 1852 at 15y 4m 4d.

P 2   WHODE, O. Michael, d. 7 May 1796 at 14y 3d. [fieldstone]

I 14   WIARD, Maria, wife of Jonathan WIARD, d. 15 Mar 1882 at 72y 1m 5d.

G 8   WIARD, Mary A., 1836 - 1914.

EE 16   WIARD, Mary, wife of Michael WIARD, d. 18 May 1869 at 65y 1m 15d.

EE 17   WIARD, Michael, 22 Dec 1889 at 92y 7m 9d.

J 13   WIAT, Ephraim, son of Jonathan & Ann WIAT, b. 25 May 1839, d. 23 May 1858 at
            18y 11m 29d.

I 13   WIAT, Jacob W., husband of Emma HEAD, b. 25 May 1829, d. 27 Jun 1868 at 29y 1m 2d.

I 12   WIAT, Jonathan, b. 28 Jun 1808, d. 8 Aug 1861 at 53y 1m 11d.

R 13   WILKINSON, Jane Flood, b. 7 Sep 1800, d. 16 Nov 1869.

R 7   WILKINSON, Thomas, d. 18 Sep 1843 at 73y 7m.

N 1   WILLIAMS, Ann Amelia, wife of Israel WILLIAMS, b. 29 Apr 1790, d. 4 Mar 1874.

X 14   WILLIAMS, Ann M., wife of H. S. WILLIAMS, b. 1 Sep 1821, d. 10 Mar 1889.

P 13   WILLIAMS, Ann R., daughter of T. K. & Sarah A. WILLIAMS, d. 4 Aug 1850 at 13m 26d.

F 9   WILLIAMS, Elizabeth, b. 31 Mar 1815, d. 1 Jun 1893 at 78y 2m 4d.

Pile   WILLIAMS, F. P., son of H. S. & M. A. WILLIAMS, b. 7 Jul 1853, d. 4 Oct 1876 at 23y 2m 27d.

X 11   WILLIAMS, Henry S., son of Israel, d. 10 May 1872 at 53 yrs.

O 1   WILLIAMS, Israel Samuel, son of Israel & Permelia WILLIAMS, b. 25 Jul 1825,
            d. 25 Mar 1842.

N 2   WILLIAMS, Israel, b. 20 Dec 1784, d. 20 Sep 1845 at 60y 9m.

F 10   WILLIAMS, John C., b. 23 Nov 1815, d. 3 Jan 1899.

F 11   WILLIAMS, John C., son of Joseph J. & Sophia C. WILLIAMS, d. 4 Apr 1899 at 25y 2m 20d.

F 13   WILLIAMS, Sarah M., b. 6 Jan 1838, d. 23 Feb 1917.

F 12   WILLIAMS, Sophia C., wife of Joseph J. WILLIAMS, d. 1 Mar 1904 at 64y 1m.

U 33   WILT, Anna E., b. 7 Jul 1851, d. 4 Sep 1916.

U 33   WILT, Edna P., b. 9 Apr 1885, d. 5 Aug 1918.

W 22   WILT, Samuel Franklin, son of Daisy E. & J. F. WILT, b. 3 Dec 1908, d. 17 Dec 1913 at 5y 14d.

U 32   WILT, T. Franklin, 1848 - 1933.

N 6   WINCE, Philip, b. 1779, d. 1842 at 64 yrs.

X 1   WINE, Catherine, wife of Jacob WINE, b. 24 Mar 1755, d. 25 Aug 1826 at 71y 5m 1d.

AA 1   WINE, Jacob, b. 6 Oct 1757, d. 11 Oct 1823 at 60y 5d.

R 2   WINSEL, Catherine, wife of George WINSEL, b. 6 Jan 1771, d. 11 Aug 1831 at 60y 8m 7d.

U 5   WINSEL, Charlotte Elizabeth, daughter of Philip & Elizabeth WINSEL, b. 9 Oct 1831,
           d. 11 Mar 1832 at 1y 4m 22d.

R 4   WINSEL, George Stephen, son of Philip & Louisa WINSEL, d. 7 Oct 1841 at 1y 4m 18d.

T 7   WINCEL, John, d. 1837 at 1y 25d.

U 6   WINSEL, John Phillip, d. 21 Aug 1836 at 6d.

N 22   WIRE, J. Clinton, son of George & Sarah L. WIRE, b. 27 Sep 1858, d. 22 Nov 1863 at
           5y 1m 25d.

N 21   WIRE, William Franklin, son of George & Sarah Ann WIRE, b. 18 Apr 1856, d. 21 Oct 1857 at
           1y 6m 13d.

Q 1   WIRTS, John H., d. 20 Dec 1835 at 10y 10m 27d.

Y 4   WIRTS, Margaret, daughter of Peter & Christine WIRTS, d. 24 Mar 1870 at 68 yrs.

P 5   WIRTS, Mary, d. 20 Dec 1837 at 1y 4m 16d.

QQ 1   WIRTS, Peter, b. 9 Dec 1812, d. 1 Nov 1868 at 55y 10m 22d.

DD 1   WIRTS, Sarah P., daughter of Peter & Christine WIRTS, d. 28 Apr 1876 at 63yrs.

T 4   WIRTZ, Jacob, d. 7 Apr 1829 at 60y 10m 12d.

O 2   WIRTZ, John, d. 28 May 1841 at 32 yrs.

T 3   WIRTZ, Lucy, wife of Jacob WIRTZ, d. 20 Nov 1825 at 37 yrs.

II 1   WIRTZ, William, b. 23 Dec 1792, d. 29 Sep 1878 at 85y 9m 6d.

KK 4   WIRZ, Willem, d. 1782. [fieldstone]

KK 3   WIZE, Peter, d. 22 May 1798 at 60y 1m 9d.

II 2   WIZES, Catherine, d. 10 Aug 1804 at 36y 4m.

II 2   WIZES, infant at 10m.

II 2   WIZES, Mical at 44yrs.

Q 15   WOLFORD, Susannah, b. 5 Jul 1785, d. 19 Jun 1869.

L 12   WOLFORD, William, d. 2 Jun 1849 at 76 yrs.

V 5   WOOD, Jessie Lee, b. 9 Jun 1893, d. 30 Jun 1943.

EE 15   WORDSWORTH, Mary F., daughter of Lewis & Catherine WORDSWORTH,
           d. 23 Aug 1850 at 9m 28d.

List   WRIGHT, Daisy, daughter of S. J. & A. S. WRIGHT, d. 11 Jan 1883.

BB 21   WRIGHT, Lizzie Chilettie, daughter of Samuel F. & Margaret H. A. WRIGHT,
d. 30 Oct 1881 at 6y 9m 9d.

FF 12   YAKEY, Anna M., 6 Mar 1786, d. 15 Jan 1870.

FF 8   –RY, Margaret, consort of [broken]

NN 6   –W C– [fieldstone]

ROW ORDER LIST

[front of cemetery, near church]

A 1   COOPER, Thomas J., b. 4 Nov 1853, d. 12 Apr 1918.

B 1   COOPER, Esther V., b. 19 Aug 1850, d. 9 Jun 1906.

B 2   COOPER, Benjamin F., b. 13 Jun 1856, d. 26 Dec 1917.

B 3   COOPER, Mary S., b. 5 Jun 1856, d. 9 Dec 1932.

C 1   LEWIS, Caroline E., b. 25 Jul 1830, d. 14 May 1898.

C 1   LEWIS, Robert S., b. 31 Jul 1825, d. 27 Aug 1905.

C 2   STREAM, Jacob H., d. 27 Sep 1904, at 72 y 1m 17d.

C 3   ENGLISH, Ellen O., b. 16 Mar 1847, d. 22 Jun 1917.

C 4   ENGLISH, William T., b. 21 Jun 1840, d. 13 Aug 1912.

C 5   HAWES, Charles R., b. 9 Jun 1891, d. 1 Dec 1940.

D 1   CRIM, Susan C., wife of Armistead CRIM, d. 28 Aug 1890 at 54y 5m 11d.

D 2   ORME, Robert S., son of Archibald & Etta ORME, d. 21 Jan 1884 at 74y 4m 15d.

D 3   FRY, John P., d. 4 Oct 1888 at 55y 7m 22d.

D 4   COOPER, George, b. 9 Mar 1820, d. 16 Dec 1892.

D 4   COOPER, Mary C., wife of George COOPER, b. 24 Mar 1833, d. 1 Jan 1897.

D 5   HEFFNER, Sarah, wife of John HEFFNER, d. 19 Nov 1895 at 87y 9m 4d.

E 1   FRY, Elizabeth, d. 9 Oct 1890, at 60y 7m 8d.

E 2   ARNOLD, Martha A., wife of Joseph ARNOLD, d. 26 Jun 1880 at 74 yrs.

E 3   SHUMAKER, John, b. 6 Nov 1796, d. 14 May 1881 at 84y 6m 8d.

E 4   SHUMAKER, Catherine, b. 16 Jan 1807, d. 3 Jan 1894 at 86y 11m 17d.

E 5   FRY, John H., b. 25 Mar 1832, d. 27 May 1881 at 49y 2m 2d.

E 6   FRY, Elizabeth, d. 15 Mar 1888 at 79y 11m 15d.

E 7   COOPER, Emeline, b. 18 Apr 1818, d. 1 Jun 1881 at 63y 1m 13d.

E 8   SHUMAKER, Margaret, b. 16 Aug 1824, d. 11 May 1882.

E 9   GREEN, L. Estella, b. 6 Apr 1873, d. 10 May 1926.

F 1   FRY, Peter, d. 26 Feb 1879 at 78y 4m 7d.

F 2   FRYE, Catherine A., daughter of Elizabeth FRYE, b. 8 Mar 1856, d. 7 May 1876.

F 3   ARNOLD, Joseph, b. 4 Dec 1819, d. 12 Dec 1878.

F 4   FRY, William, b. 30 Nov 1806, d. 11 May 1879.

F 5   WERKING, George, b. 18 Feb 1822, d. 19 May 1879 at 52y 8m 1d.

F 6   SHUMAKER, Mary, d. 1 Jun 1879 at 68y 3m 11d.

F 7   SPRING, Charlott, d. 26 May 1880 at 81 yrs.

F 8   HEFFNER, John, d. 6 Dec 1880 at 78y 3m 7d.

F 9   WILLIAMS, Elizabeth, b. 31 Mar 1815, d. 1 Jun 1893 at 78y 2m 4d.

F 10   WILLIAMS, John C., b. 23 Nov 1815, d. 3 Jan 1899.

F 11   WILLIAMS, John C., son of Joseph J. & Sophia C. WILLIAMS, d. 4 Apr 1899 at 25y 2m 20d.

F 12   WILLIAMS, Sophia C., wife of Joseph J. WILLIAMS, d. 1 Mar 1904 at 64y 1m.

F 13   WILLIAMS, Sarah M., b. 6 Jan 1838, d. 23 Feb 1917.

G 1   HEFFNER, Elizabeth, wife of Frederick HEFFNER, d. 24 Jan 1874 at 78y 3m 16d.

G 2   FRY, Angeline, b. 27 Jul 1824, d. 6 Mar 1875.

G 3   ORME, Eliza A., wife of Robert S. ORME, b. 22 Feb 1812, d. 1 Jan 1876 at 63y 10m 9d.

G 4   VINCEL, George, d. 21 Oct 1876 at 71y 4m.

G 5   VINCEL, Catharine, wife of George VINCEL, d. 27 Nov 1894 at 86y 11d.

G 6   MANN, Sarah, wife of John MANN, d. 5 Apr 1810, d. 10 Mar 1877.

G 7   MANN, Ida A., daughter of George & Leanna MANN, d. 15 May 1862 at 9y 22d.

G 8   WIARD, Mary A., 1836 - 1914.

G 9   SPINKS, James, Lizzie, Amie, Mamie, Mary [no dates]

H 1   KERN, William, d. 19 Jul 1885 at 77y 3m 3d.

H 2   KERN, Jacob, b. 15 Aug 1776, d. 29 Aug 1860 at 84y 24d.

H 3   KERN, Elizabeth, b. 12 Nov 1781, d. 6 Dec 1861 at 80y 25d.

H 4   FRY, Susannah, daughter of Michael & Susannah FRY, b. 6 May 1823, d. 15 Sep 1860.

H 5   KADEL, Anna C., wife of Peter COMPHER, b. 28 May 1785, d. 9 Oct 1860.

H 6   HICKMAN, Catharine M., daughter of George & Eleanor HICKMAN, d. 11 Nov 1860 at 2y 3m 12d.

H 7   VIRTS, Henry, 1822 - 1861.

H 7   VIRTS, Virginia, 1829 - 1902.

H 8   ARNOLD, Jacob, d. 5 Oct 1861 at 74 yrs.

H 9   ARNOLD, Mary, wife of Jacob ARNOLD, d. 28 Jan 1865 at 71y 2m 28d.

H 10   MANN, Charity, daughter of Edward & Flora MORRISON, b. 23 Oct 1833, d. 24 Sep 1860 at
        26y 11m 1d.

H 11   RUST, Margaret A., wife of James W. RUST, d. 4 Dec 1861 at 38y 1m 29d.

H 12   HICKMAN, Mary E., wife of Peter HICKMAN, b. 25 Mar 1825, d. 9 Jan 1862.

H 13   HICKMAN, Peter, b. 14 Aug 1818, d. 9 Sep 1863 at 45y 19d.

H 14   HICKMAN, Catharine, d. 6 Jun 1869 at 54y 5m 5d.

I 1   LUCKETT, Samuel C., b. 6 Nov 1807, d. 7 Aug 1893 at 85y 9m 1d.

I 2   MANN, George William, b. 24 Jul 1819, d. 13 Apr 1858 at 38y 8m 20d.

I 3   HOUSEHOLDER, George W., son of the late Gideon HOUSEHOLDER, b. 8 Dec 1841,
        d. 14 Jan 1859 at 17y 1m 6d.

I 4   ARNOLD, Elizabeth P., consort of John ARNOLD, d. 29 Apr 1859 at 39y 1m 15d.

I 5   POTTERFIELD, Elizabeth, relict of Jacob POTTERFIELD , d. 31 July 1859 at
        79y 4m 16d. [broken]

I 6   HOUSEHOLDER, Catharine, wife of Jacob HOUSEHOLDER, b. 14 Aug 1817, d. 16 Aug 1859
        at 42y 2d.

I 7   JACOBS, Wm. H., d. 7 Sep 1859 at 62 yrs.

I 8   HICKMAN, Mary E., daughter of Peter & Mary C. HICKMAN, b. 21 Mar 1859,
        d. 11 Dec 1859.

I 9   COOPER, Julius Tilghman, b. 10 Oct 1852, d. 23 Jan 1860.

I 10   FAWLEY, Henry, b. 4 Mar 1784, d. 2 Jul 1860 at 76y 3m 28d.

I 11   FAWLEY, Christena, wife of Henry FAWLEY, b. 18 May 1786, d. 9 Jan 1861 at 74y 7m 21d.

I 12   WIAT, Jonathan, b. 28 Jun 1808, d. 8 Aug 1861 at 53y 1m 11d.

I 13   WIAT, Jacob W., husband of Emma HEAD, b. 25 May 1829, d. 27 Jun 1868 at 29y 1m 2d.

I 14   WIARD, Maria, wife of Jonathan WIARD, d. 15 Mar 1882 at 72y 1m 5d.

I 15   ARNOLD, John, b. 5 Aug 1816, d. 1 Jan 1902.

I 15   COPELAND, Mary C., b. 18 Feb 1846, d. 20 Mar 1909.

I 15   DONALDSON, Robert B., b. 7 Apr 1878, d. 31 Aug 1910.

I 15   DONALDSON, Walter S., b. 1 Jan 1829, d. 23 Nov 1884.

I 16   FRY, Elizabeth C., b. 24 Mar 1847, d. 18 Oct 1904.

I 16   FRY, Philip, b. 3 Feb 1820, d. 25 Jun 1902.

J 1   LUCKETT, Mary B., daughter of Samuel C. & Mary B. LUCKETT, b. 26 Nov 1846,
        d. 16 Mar 1890.

J 2   SLATER, Catherine, consort of Jacob SLATER, b. 1 Jan 1769, d. 13 Apr 1857.

J 3   COMPHER, Mary, daughter of John & Elizabeth COMPHER, b. 20 Sep 1810, d. 29 Oct 1854
        at 44y 1m 9d.

J 4   COMPHER, Anna Mary, wife of William COMPHER, and daughter of Henry & Christina
        FAWLEY, b. 6 Sep 1814, d. 20 Sep 1854.

J 5   FRY, Andrew, b. 20 Oct 1790, d. 12 Aug 1854 at 63y 21m 11d.

J 6   COOPER, Solomon, b. 8 Nov 1803, d. 2 Aug 1855 at 51y 8m.

J 7   RUSE, Annie E., wife of Edward S. RUSE, and only daughter of the late George SLATER,
        b. 20 Feb 1835, d. 20 Dec 1855 at 20y 10m.

J 8   HICKMAN, Catharine Amanda, daughter of Peter & Mary E. HICKMAN, b. 21 Nov 1847,
        d. 21 Apr 1856 at 8y 4m 27d.

J 9   COOPER, Eve Ann, wife of John COOPER, b. 29 Mar 1882, d. 28 Apr 1856 at 71y 30d.

J 10   LUCKETT, Charles W. [sunken]

J 11   COOPER, John, Sr., b. 29 Feb 1782, d. 10 Nov 1856 at 74y 8m 10d.

J 12   MORRISON, Edward, b. 22 Jun 1785, d. 13 Apr 1858 at 72y 9m 21d.

J 13   WIAT, Ephraim, son of Jonathan & Ann WIAT, b. 25 May 1839, d. 23 May 1858 at
        18y 11m 29d.

J 14   VINCEL, Margaret Jane, daughter of Solomon & Louisa VINCEL, b. 15 Apr 1845,
        d. 13 Jun 1858.

J 15   EVERHART, Eliza A., d. 11 Feb 1857 at 40y 16d.

J 16   OREM, Mary P., wife of Nathanel OREM, d. 28 Nov 1882 at 32y 1 m 4d.

J 17   ARNOLD, Charles W., d. 8 Aug 1882 at 27 yrs.

J 18   COOPER, son of R. H. & A. P. COOPER

K 1   SLATER, Ann Eliza, wife of Samuel W. SLATER, daughter of Samuel & Mary
        STOUTSENBERGER, b. 26 Jul 1836, d. 3 Mar 1857.

K 2   HOUGH, Samuel Hampton, son of Charles K. & Ara O. HOUGH, b. 9 Mar 1849,
        d. 26 Apr 1854 at 5y 1m 17d.

K 3   HOUGH, Charles K., b. 4 Jul 1823, d. 20 Sep 1853 at 30y 2m 16d.

K 4   SLATER, Barbary, wife of Samuel SLATER, b. 1 Aug 1808, d. 20 Aug 1854 at 46y 19d.

K 5   MYERS, Sarah Jane, daughter of William & Catherine MYERS, b. 28 Feb 1851,
            d. 30 Sep 1854 at 3y 7m 2d.

K 6   COMPHER, Samuel Edward, son of Wm. & E. COMPHER, b. 28 Jun 1854, d. 17 Sep 1854
            at 2m 19d.

K 6   COMPHER, William, b. 3 Feb 1812, d. 16 Sep 1854.

K 7   HOUSEHOLDER, Hamilton, b. 11 Nov 1826, d. 23 Feb 1853.

K 8   HAMILTON, Caroline Amanda, wife of James W. HAMILTON, daughter of Gideon
            HOUSEHOLDER, b. 29 Nov 1823, d. 1 Mar 1853.

K 9   WHITE, Elizabeth, daughter of William & Maria WHITE, b. 22 Oct 1821, d. 28 Aug 1854 at
            29y 10m 6d.

K 10   LUCKETT, Mary B., wife of Samuel C. LUCKETT, b. 14 May 1809, d. 9 Oct 1853.

K 11   BEAMER, Julia Ann, wife of Michael BEAMER, b. 16 Jun 1815, d. 20 Oct 1852 at 27y 4m 4d.

K 12   BEAMER, Mary Elizabeth, wife of James W. BEAMER, d. 19 Nov 1853 at 22y 2m 2d.

K 13   SNOOTS, John, b. 21 Oct 1838, d. 22 Sep 1854 at 15y 10m 29d.

K 14   HOUGH, Mary Ann, wife of John HOUGH, b. 26 May 1823, d. 28 Sep 1854.

K 15   MILLER, Nancy, d. 30 Dec 1851 at 73 yrs.

K 16   MANN, Jacob F., son of Joseph & Elizabeth MANN, b. 25 Nov 1839, d. 20 Jun 1858 at
            18y 6m 25 d.

K 17   MARCHE, Anna L., d. 26 Jun 1867 at 1y 7d.

K 17   REED, Charles A., d. Feb 1864 at 14 yrs.

K 18   JOHNSON, Lydia Jane, wife of Henry A. JOHNSON, b. 5 Jan 1834, d. 15 Feb 1860.

K 19   LEWIS, infant of Charles M. & Elizabeth LEWIS

K 20   LEWIS, Charles M., b. 20 May 1840, d. 22 Oct 1863 at 23y 5m 2d.

K 21   WENNER, Alberta Alder, daughter of Jonathan & Mary C. WENNER, d. 25 Jun 1871
            at 5m 9d.

K 21   WENNER, Jonathan A., d. 13 Oct 1882 at 41y 5m.

K 21   WENNER, Mary C., wife of Jonathan A. WENNER, b. 27 Sep 1841, d. 16 Aug 1916.

K 22   CASE, Mabel Amelia, daughter of G. W. & Rose B. CASE, d. 4 Jul 1890 at 11m 5d.

K 23   LEE, Julia Ettie, b. 3 Apr 1846, d. 14 Oct 1911.

L 1   ARNOLD, Martin L., b. 10 Sep 1820, d. 13 Feb 1853 at 32y 5m 3d.

L 2   MANN, Anna Maria, wife of John MANN, b. 4 May 1775, d. 3 May 1859 at 83y 11m 30d.

L 3   TRITAPOE, John H., son of Charles & L. A. TRITAPOE, b. 2 Apr 1866, d. 4 Aug 1867 at 1y
          4m 2d.

L 4   MANN, John, d. 22 May 1851 at 83y 3m 18d.

L 5   HAURER, Henrietta Warner, daughter of Daniel J. & Henrietta HAURER, d. 18 Aug 1842 at
          5y 8m 4d.

L 6   AXLINE, David, b. 17 Feb 1772, d. 9 Nov 1844 at 72y 8m 22d.

L 7   AXLINE, Eve, wife of David AXLINE, b. 6 May 1776, d. 4 Jul 1854.

L 8   HOUSEHOLDER, Caroline M., consort of Hamilton HOUSEHOLDER, b. 29 Sep 1827,
          d. 1 Sep 1849 at 21y 11m 2d.

L 9   AXLINE, Catharine S., consort of David AXLINE, b. 27 Nov 1816, d. 24 Nov 1849 at
          32y 11m 27d.

L 10   WHITE, Rebecca, d. 14 May 1850 at 23 yrs.

L 11   LUCKETT, Luther C., b. 9 Sep 1818, d. 31 May 1844 at 25y 8m 22d.

L 12   WOLFORD, William, d. 2 Jun 1849 at 76 yrs.

L 13   SMITH, Mary, b. 29 Jul 1799, d. 25 Aug 1851.

L 14   COOPER, William Washington, , son of John & Sarah COOPER, b. 7 Jan 1831, d. 26 Jun 1845
          at 14y 5m 19d.

L 15   COOPER, Henry Clay, son of John & Sarah COOPER, b. 9 Dec 1844. [no death date]

L 16   JACOBS, Sarah Catharine Wise, daughter of William H. & Catharine JACOBS,
          d. 14 Mar 1843 at 1y 11m 12d.

L 17   JACOBS, Eliza Elinor, daughter of William H. & Catharine JACOBS, d. 5 Jul 1842 at
          5y 1m 25d.

L 18   STONEBURNER, infant son of J. C. & C. E. STONEBURNER, d. 3 Dec 1855.

L 19   VICKERS, Josephine L., d. 10 May 1856, 1y 11m 22d.

L 20   LEWIS, Laura F., daughter of Robert A. & Caroline M. LEWIS, b. 30 Nov 1851, d. 16 Jun 1876.

L 21   HUNTER, infant daughter of Michael & Marguretta HUNTER, b. & d. 1 Sep 1877.

L 22   BOGER, Mary E., daughter of Samuel & Mary BOGER, b. 25 Jun 1854, d. 4 Aug 1857 at
          3y 1m 9d.

L 23   GRAHAM, George H., son of John & Mary GRAHAM, d. 4 Jan 1868 at 1y 10m 4d.

L 23   GRAHAM, Lydia E., daughter of John & Mary GRAHAM, d. 16 Nov 1864 at 3y 6m 20d.

L 23   GRAHAM, Mary C., daughter of John & Mary GRAHAM, d. 22 Sep 1857 at 1m 15d.

L 24   VIRTS, Willie, infant son of William H. & Marietta VIRTS, d. 17 Apr 1872 at 9d.

L 25   ENGLISH, Hauer Chester, son of W. T. & E. O. ENGLISH, b. 21 Jan 1872 at 9d.

L 26   ENGLISH, Lucy E., infant of W. T. & E. O. ENGLISH, d. 24 Jun 1890.

L 27   VICKERS, Eunice A., daughter of Richard & J. T. VICKERS, b. 14 Nov 1879, d. 20 Dec 1879.

[first stone is 60 feet from fence]

M 1   STUCK, Mary M., d. 18 Jul 1851 at 41y 21d.

M 2   FAWLEY, Sally Gertrude, daughter of William & Elizabeth FAWLEY, b. 30 Nov 1856,
        d. 23 Dec 1859 at 3y 23d.

M 3   FAWLEY, Sarah E., daughter of William & Elizabeth FAWLEY, b. 2 Apr 1842,
        d. 1 Aug 1845.

M 4   STONEBURNER, Laura Jane, daughter of Peter & Catherine STONEBURNER,
        d. 22 Sep 1851 at 2y 8d.

M 5   SNOOTS, Susan R., daughter of John & Anna J. SNOOTS, b. 22 Sep 1853, d. 9 Nov 1854 at
        1y 1m 18d.

M 6   SPEAKS, Margaret C. A., daughter of Richard & Mary E. SPEAKS, b. 6 Sep 1855,
        d. 27 Nov 1855 at 2m 21d.

M 7   BARTLETT, Adah Virginia, daughter of Nathaniel & Margaret BARTLETT, b. 26 Dec 1868,
        d. 23 Aug 1870.

N 1   WILLIAMS, Ann Amelia, wife of Israel WILLIAMS, b. 29 Apr 1790, d. 4 Mar 1874.

N 2   WILLIAMS, Israel, b. 20 Dec 1784, d. 20 Sep 1845 at 60y 9m.

N 3   ARNOLD, Noah, b. 27 Apr 1817, d. 7 Jun 1850 at 33y 1m 10d.

N 4   ARNOLD, David, b. 21 Sep 1814, d. 6 Jul 1842 at 27y 9m 15d.

N 5   ARNOLD, Sophia Matilda, daughter of Noah & Emiline ARNOLD, b. 14 Oct 1841,
        d. 31 Aug 1854 at 12y 10m 17d.

N 6   WINCE, Philip, b. 1779, d. 1842 at 64 yrs.

N 7   VINCEL, Solomon, b. 27 Jul 1808, d. 29 Oct 1854 at 46y 3m 2d.

N 8   GOODHART, Mary, wife of Jacob GOODHART, daughter of John FAWLEY, d. 4 Sep 1853 at
        65y 10m 11d.

N 9   GOODHART, Jacob, d. 12 Apr 1843 at 57y 9m 12d.

N 10   FAWLEY, John, d. 15 July 1850 at 89y 10m 3d.

N 11   COOPER, Philip, b. 8 Oct 1775, d. 13 Jun 1843 at 67y 8m 5d.

N 12   MANN, Joannah Elizabeth, daughter of Joseph & Elizabeth MANN, b. 27 Sep 1836,
                    d. 2 Oct 1845.

N 13   VIRTS, Leah, wife of Peter VIRTS, b. 15 May 1812, d. 14 Sep 1849 at 36y 4m.

N 14   COOPER, Elizabeth E., wife of Philip COOPER, b. 4 Mar 1777, d. 30 Jul 1863 at 86y 4m 26d.

N 15   COOPER, Mary, wife of George COOPER, b. 12 Aug 1774, d. 16 Feb 1858 at 83y 6m 4d.

N 16   COOPER, George, b. 14 Feb 1770, d. 18 Aug 1846 at 76y 6m 4d.

N 17   WENNER, Sarah, relict of John WENNER, d. 16 May 1850 at 49y 8m 4d.

N 18   STUCK, Peter, b. 20 Sep 1766, d. 4 May 1846 at 79y 7m 14d.

N 19   STUCK, Elizabeth, b. 13 Mar 1773, d. 7 Aug 1850 at 77y 4m 24d.

N 20   VINCEL, George T., d. 5 Sep 1856 at 34y 6m.

N 21   WIRE, William Franklin, son of George & Sarah Ann WIRE, b. 18 Apr 1856, d. 21 Oct 1857 at
                    1y 6m 13d.

N 22   WIRE, J. Clinton, son of George & Sarah L. WIRE, b. 27 Sep 1858, d. 22 Nov 1863 at
                    5y 1m 25d.

[first stone is 6 feet from fence]

O 1   WILLIAMS, Israel Samuel, son of Israel & Permelia WILLIAMS, b. 25 Jul 1825,
                    d. 25 Mar 1842.

O 2   WIRTZ, John, d. 28 May 1841 at 32 yrs.

O 3   EVERHART, Susan Manzilla, daughter of John & Mary E. EVERHART, b. 12 Sep 1853,
                    d. 26 Aug 1854.

P 1   FAWLEY, Margaret, wife of John FAWLEY, d. at 76 yrs.

P 2   WHODE, O. Michael, d. 7 May 1796 at 14y 3d. [fieldstone]

P 3   STOUTSENBERGER, Maria M., relict of John STOUTSENBERGER, d. 9 Oct 1847 at
                    85y 5m 23d.

P 4   STOUTSENBERGER, John, b. 2 Apr 1762, d. 31 Mar 1837 at 74y 11m 29d.

P 5   WIRTS, Mary, d. 20 Dec 1837 at 1y 4m 16d.

P 6   EVERHART, Michael, b. 29 Sep 1772, d. 14 Jan 1853.

P 7   EVERHART, Christina, wife of Michael EVERHART, d. 18 Jun 1846 at 66y 7m 18d.

P 8   SHAFER, John, d. 10 Mar 1838 at 72 yrs.

P 9   SHAFFER, John William, son of Joseph B. & Susan SHAFFER, b. 11 Oct 1852, d. 16 Apr 1853
                    at 6m 2d.

P 10   SHAFFER, Mary, d. 22 Apr 1842 at 75 yrs.

P 11   SHAFFER, John, b. 1 Mar 1807, d. 10 Sep 1843 at 36y 3m 9d.

P 12   SPRING, Lydia Ann, consort of Elias SPRING, b. 22 Dec 1830, d. 28 Dec 1847 at 17y 6d.

P 13   WILLIAMS, Ann R., daughter of T. K. & Sarah A. WILLIAMS, d. 4 Aug 1850 at 13m 26d.

P 14   MANN, Peter Silas, son of John & Sarah MANN, b. 1 Nov 1826, d. 11 Sep 1850.

P 15   COMPHER, Sarah, d. 24 Apr 1842 at 5 yrs.

P 16   COMPHER, Esther Ann, consort of John COMPHER, b. 2 Sep 1823, d. 25 Sep 1846 at 23y 23d.

[first stone is 30 feet from fence]

Q 1   WIRTS, John H., d. 20 Dec 1835 at 10y 10m 27d.

[space of 20 feet]

Q 2   ROPP, William M., son of Samuel & Rachel ROPP, b. 29 Aug 1845, d. 19 Aug 1846.

Q 3   HAMILTON, Susan Elizabeth, daughter of James W. & Caroline A. HAMILTON,
        b. 14 Feb 1848, d. 2 Apr 1851.

Q 4   HOUSEHOLDER, Gideon, b. 5 Nov 1800, d. 15 Sep 1845 at 44y 10m 10d.

Q 5   HOUSEHOLDER, Julia Ann, wife of Gideon HOUSEHOLDER, b. 8 Jun 1801, d. 7 Sep 1848 at
        47y 2m 29d.

Q 6   BEAMER, Peter, son of Geo. & Catharine BEAMER, b. 22 Jan 1821, d. 8 Jul 1845 at 21y 5m 16d.

Q 7   ROLLER, John, b. 11 Dec 1781, d. 30 May 1843 at 61y 5m 19d.

Q 8   VIRTS, Phebe, wife of W. VIRTS, d. 29 Apr 1845 at 57 yrs.

Q 9   EAMICH, John, b. Apr 1783, d. 7 Jan 1845 at 62y 9m.

Q 10   EDWARDS, George W., son of Thomas M. & Sarah EDWARDS, b. 20 Mar 1861, d. 16 Jun 1862
        at 1y 2m 26d.

Q 11   EDWARDS, Jonathan, d. 5 Apr 1873 at 41y 3m 12d.

Q 12   HART, Emma Jane, daughter of Joseph & Rachael A. HART, b. 14 Feb 1858, d. 30 Jun 1858 at
        4m 16d.

Q 13   BARTLETT, Alice M., daughter of John W. & Elizabeth BARTLETT, d. 18 Aug 1867 at
        2m 27d.

Q 14   WENNER, Lydia Jane, daughter of J. W. & L. WENNER, d. 31 Mar 1869 at 21y 5m 5d.

Q 15   WOLFORD, Susannah, b. 5 Jul 1785, d. 19 Jun 1869.

Q 16   SCHAEFFER, Jacob, d. 3 Dec 1873 at 69y 7m.

Q 17   SCHAFFER, Henry, d. 4 Nov 1876 at 76yrs.

Q 18   SCHAEFFER, Malinda, daughter of Jacob SCHAEFFER, d. 2 Feb 1879 at 70y 11m 8d.

[first stone is 20 feet from fence]

R 1   FILLER, Henry, b. 12 Dec 1801, d. 22 Jul 1831 at 29y 7m 10d.

R 2   WINSEL, Catherine, wife of George WINSEL, b. 6 Jan 1771, d. 11 Aug 1831 at 60y 8m 7d.

R 3   VINCEL, Mary C., daughter of Philip & Louisa VINCEL, b. 3 Oct 1828, d. 28 Nov 1847 at
        19y 1m 25d.

R 4   WINSEL, George Stephen, son of Philip & Louisa WINSEL, d. 7 Oct 1841 at 1y 4m 18d.

R 5   AXLINE, Henry Harrison, son of Emanuel & Susan AXLINE, d. 29 Aug 1840, d. 7 Nov 1846 at
        6y 2m 8d.

R 6   BEAMER, Infant son of James W. & Mary Elizabeth BEAMER, b. 23 Oct 1853, d. 9 Nov 1853
        at 15d.

R 7   WILKINSON, Thomas, d. 18 Sep 1843 at 73y 7m.

R 8   COMPHER, Mariah E., wife of John COMPHER, d. 19 May 1862 at 77y 9m 22d.

R 9   HICKMAN, Catharine, wife of John HICKMAN, b. 20 Sep 1792, d. 1 Aug 1862 at
        69y 10m 12d.

R 10   ARNOLD, Michael, d. 11 May 1863 at 72y 8m 5d.

R 11   RUST, James W., b. 11 Dec 1819, d. 28 Feb 1866 at 46y 2m 12d.

R 12   WENNER, William C., son of J. W. & L. WENNER, d. 5 Oct 1870 at 1y 2m 22d.

R 13   WILKINSON, Jane Flood, b. 7 Sep 1800, d. 16 Nov 1869.

R 14   FRY, Elizabeth, wife of Andrew FRY, d. 5 Jun 1873 at 80y 8m 4m.

R 15   TRITAPOE, Michael, d. 4 Jul 1873 at 75y 2m 8d.

S 1   COMPHER, John, Sr., b. 4 Dec 1773, d. 24 Apr 1846 at 72y 4m 20d.

S 2   COOPER, Mary E., wife of Adam COOPER, b. 25 May 1833, d. 10 Jan 1892.

S 3   COLLINS, Margaret A., d. 30 Oct 1888 at 76y 3m 5d.

S 4   COOPER, George F., son of Fredrick C., b. 6 Aug 1792, d. 25 Aug 1833 at 41y 19d.

S 5   SHAFFER, Lucinda, d. 1 Jan 1833 at 18y 10m 19d.

S 6   SHAFFER, Christena, d. 23 Apr 1833 at 22y 3m 12d.

S 7   SCHAFFER, Mary Elizabeth, b. 13 Apr 1835 at 64y 6m 8d. [illegible]

S 8   SHAFFER, Henry, d. 1 Jan 1832 at 38y 1m 23d.

S 9   VINCEL, Mary M., b. 26 Jul 1766, d. 17 Sep 1846 at 80y 1m 21d.

S 10   VINSEL, John, Sr., b. 10 Jan 1764, d. 27 Mar 1835 at 71 yrs.

S 11   BELSO, Frederic, d. 19 Jan 1831 at 88 yrs.

S 12   AXLINE, Silas A., d. 13 Mar 1838 at 15m.

S 13   AXLINE, Samuel V., son of Emanuel AXLINE, d. 3 Sep 1838 at 4y 2m 12d.

S 14   AXLINE, William T., son of Emanuel & Susannah AXLINE, d. 3 Aug 1829 at 5y 3m 17d.

S 15   AXLINE, Gideon, son of John AXLINE, d. 17 Nov 1826 at 7y 10m 20d.

S 16   SLATER, Catherine, infant child of William & Margaret SLATER, d. 12 Feb 1835.

S 17   SLATER, Mary, daughter of William & Margaret SLATER, d. 5 Dec 184– [broken] at 6yrs.

S 18   KALB, infant daughter of John G. R. & Ellen M. KALB, b. 25 Mar 1863.

S 19   FRY, Julius F., son of Noah & Susannah FRY, d. 12 Oct 1855.

S 20   FRYE, infant son of Noah & Susannah FRYE, d. 11 Oct 1852.

S 21   RICHARSON, H. M. M., infant son of Rev. X. J. & M. I. RICHARDSON, d. 4 Jan 1865 at 16d.

S 22   FRY, Margaret A., b. 20 Nov 1813, d. 2 Aug 1899 at 85y 8m 12d.

[first stone is 25 feet from fence]

T 1   SACKMAN, Sarah, d. 10 Feb 1831 at 31y 10m 23d.

T 2   SHAFFER, Michael, d. 5 Mar 1830 at 25y 13d.

T 3   WIRTZ, Lucy, wife of Jacob WIRTZ, d. 20 Nov 1825 at 37 yrs.

T 4   WIRTZ, Jacob, d. 7 Apr 1829 at 60y 10m 12d.

T 5   DERRY, Eliza, wife of Peter DERRY, d. 16 Mar 1827 at 25 yrs.

T 6   AXLINE, William T., son of Emmanuel & Susannah AXLINE, d. 21 Aug 1829 at 8y 3m 12d.

T 7   WINCEL, John, d. 1837 at 1y 25d.

T 8   CONRAD, Mary Catherine, daughter of Abner & Mary C. CONRAD, d. 17 Feb 1841 at
        2m 27d.

T 9   GRUBB, Alevia Catharine Charity, daughter of Benjamin & Rebecca GRUBB, d. 11 Jul 1843
        at 1y 8m 19d.

T 10   GRUBB, Edward Curtis, son of Benjamin & Rebecca GRUBB, d. 24 Dec 1844 at 1y 10d.

T 11   GRUBB, Rebecca, wife of Benjamin J. GRUBB, d. 31 Jan 1849 at 40y 5m 19d.

T 12   CRIM, Jacob, b. 26 Dec 1772, d. 22 May 1847 at 74y 4m 26d.

T 13   VICKERS, Catharine, wife of William VICKERS, b. 24 Oct 1811, d. 14 Aug 1847 at
        35y 9m 21d.

T 14   EVERHART, J., son of John & S. EVERHART, d. 4 Jun – at 3d.

T 15   COOPER, Mary J., wife of Adam COOPER, d. 10 Nov 1864 at 50y 7m.

T 16   COOPER, Adam, d. 28 Jun 1890 at 79y 8m 3d.

T 17   HOUSEHOLDER, Jacob, b. 27 Jun 1812, d. 2 Nov 1866.

T 18   HOUSEHOLDER, Valeria G., b. 26 Dec 1856, d. 3 Nov 1866.

T 19   HOUSEHOLDER, Virginia C., b. 23 Jan 1844, d. 27 Nov 1866.

T 20   AXLINE, Harriet A., wife of David AXLINE, b. 9 Jan 1819, d. 17 Nov 1867.

T 21   AXLINE, Sarah Jane, wife of David AXLINE, b. 14 Apr 1877 at 35y 20d.

[first stone is 40 feet from fence]

U 1   FRY, C. Catharine, wife of G. H. FRY, d. 16 Mar 1897 at 43y 1m 21d.

U 2   FRY, Georgia, infant daughter of G. H. & C. FRY, d. 27 — 1897. [broken]

U 3   CRIM, Susannah, b. 5 Jan 1790, d. 2 Jun 1857.

U 4   KALB, Charles K., son of S. A. & L. A. KALB, d. 30 Aug 1874 at 3y 11m.

U 5   WINSEL, Charlotte Elizabeth, daughter of Philip & Elizabeth WINSEL, b. 9 Oct 1831,
         d. 11 Mar 1832 at 1y 4m 22d.

U 6   WINSEL, John Phillip, d. 21 Aug 1836 at 6d.

U 7   FRY, Samuel William, son of William & – FRY, d. 11 Dec 1833 at 2m 14d.

U 8   STUCK, Joseph Henry, son of F. F. & Jane STUCK, b. 15 Oct 1823, d. 2 Oct 1841.

U 9   STUCK, Charles A., son of F. F. & Jane STUCK, b. 28 Aug 1825, d. 30 Sep 1829.

U 10   STUCK, Peter, son of F. F. & Jane STUCK, b. 4 Sep 1827, d. 14 Oct 1830.

U 11   KERN, Benjamin, d. 10 Mar 1833 at 3y 11m 10d.

U 12   KERN, Aaron J., b. 27 Mar 1819, d. 3 Apr 1819 at 17d.

U 13   GRUBB, Henry Clay, son of Benjamin J. & Rebecca GRUBB, d. 12 Jan 1841 at 4m 14d.

U 14   VICKERS, Mary Amanda, daughter of William & Catherine VICKERS, b. 11 Nov 1832,
         d. 30 Nov 1833.

U 15   CRIM, Margaret, wife of John CRIM, b. 5 Feb 1798, d. 8 Sep 1834 at 36y 6m 3d.

U 16   COMPHER, Christena, daughter of William & M. COMPHER, b. 12 Nov 1845, d. 1 Jun 1846
         at 6m 20d.

U 17   CRIM, Catharine A. E., daughter of John H. & Mary M. CRIM, d. 22 Mar 1852 at 1y 6d.

U 18   CRIM, George P., son of John H. & Mary M. CRIM, d. 18 Aug 1865 at 18y 6m 12d.

U 19   FRY, infant son of Noah & S. FRY, d. 30 Oct 1857 at 8m 26d.

U 20   FRY, infant daughter of J. H. & S. E. FRY, d. 9 Jul 1871 at 5d.

U 21   FRY, Ireneus F., son of Joseph H. & S. E. FRY, d. 28 Mar 1871 at 4y 6m 8d.

U 22   FRY, Mary, d. 18 Nov 1864 at 71y 2m.

U 23   CRIM, Mary M., wife of John H. CRIM, d. 18 Sep 1865 at 43y 4m 5d.

U 24   HICKMAN, Caroline R., b. 28 Dec 1843, d. 15 Aug 1866.

U 25   HICKMAN, George, b. 14 Sep 1816, d. 27 Aug 1866.

U 26   HICKMAN, Elenora M., b. 7 Dec 1821, d. 10 Jun 1893.

U 27   SLATER, George, d. 17 Nov 1866 at 71y 1m 18d.

U 28   FRY, Sarah E., wife of David FRY, b. 23 Oct 1830, d. 13 Mar 1867.

U 29   HICKMAN, Benjamin J., b. 30 Sep 1848, d. 26 Jan 1871 at 22y 3m 26d.

U 30   HICKMAN, Samuel P., d. 12 Mar 1921 at 75y 10d.

U 31   SLATER, Sarah, wife of George SLATER, d. 5 Sep 1878 at 79y 20d.

U 32   WILT, T. Franklin, 1848 - 1933.

U 33   WILT, Anna E., b. 7 Jul 1851, d. 4 Sep 1916.

U 33   WILT, Edna P., b. 9 Apr 1885, d. 5 Aug 1918.

[first stone is 16 feet from fence]

V 1   HOUGH , Ola V., baby, d. 10 Jan 1877 at 1m 20d. [broken]

V 2   COOPER, Aaron, d. 13 Dec 1878 at 61y 2m 25d.

V 2   COOPER, Margaret, d. 16 Jan 1918 at 91yrs.

V 3   FRY, Noah, b. 28 Nov 1828, d. 17 Aug 1903.

V 3   FRY, Susannah, b. 4 Aug 1827, d. 27 Dec 1901.

V 4   VINSEL, Adam, son of John A. VINSEL, b. 17 Feb 1790, d. 23 Aug 1827 at 36y 4m 25d.

V 5   WOOD, Jessie Lee, b. 9 Jun 1893, d. 30 Jun 1943.

V 6   AUMEN, Barbara, d. 17 Aug 1832 at 60y 8m 15d.

V 7   HICKMAN, John, d. 13 Jan 1839 at 53y 1m 4d.

V 8   ORRISON, James, son of William D. & Elizabeth ORRISON, b. 15 Oct 1842, d. 14 Oct 1845 at 3 yrs.

V 9   HICKMAN, Mary, daughter of John & Catherine HICKMAN, b. 1 Mar 1813, d. 2 Jul 1841 at 27y 1m 28d.

V 10   RUST, Catherine H., daughter of James W. & Margaret RUST, b. 13 Oct 1845, d. 23 Jan 1848 at 2y 3m 10d.

[first stone is 18 feet from fence]

W 1   MANN, infant son of J. W. & E. S. MANN, 23 Feb 1902.

W 2   FRY, Miss Lucinda, b. 1 Mar 1822, d. 1 Apr 1880.

W 3   FRY, John, b. 30 Dec 1791, d. 17 Jul 1877 at 85y 6m 17d.

W 4   FRY, Christena, b. 11 Aug 1804, d. 26 Jul 1877 at 72y 11m 15d.

W 5   COOPER, Michael L., d. 18 May 1884 at 85y 5m 22d.

W 6   COOPER, Mary A., wife of Michael L. COOPER, d. 25 Sep 1896 at 73y 3m 17d.

W 7   STONEBURNER, Daniel, b. 15 Jun 1767, d. 14 Oct 1826 at 59y 3m 29d.

W 8   STONEBURNER, Anna Mary, d. 1 Nov 1844 at 75 yrs.

W 9   FRY, Susannah, wife of Michael FRY, d. 26 Aug 1826 at 39 yrs.

W 10   FRY, Michael, b. 28 Feb 1785, d. 18 Jan 1817 at 61y 10m 20d.

W 11   MORGAN, Eliza, wife of Philip MORGAN, b. 15 Dec 1807, d. 8 Sep 1829.

W 11   MORGAN, Mary M., b. 1826, d. 1829.

W 12   FAWLEY, Jacob, d. 20 Mar 1843 at 82 yrs.

W 13   FAWLEY, George, b. 4 Feb 1804, d. 1 Jan 1815 at 10y 11m 11d.

W 14   ROPP, Rachel, wife of Samuel ROPP, b. 2 Apr 1821, d. 4 Nov 1848 at 27y 7m 2d.

W 15   VINCEL, John, son of John VINCEL, Sr., b. 3 Jan 1792, d. 27 Dec 1826.

W 16   COMPHER, Margaret, wife of Peter COMPHER, b. 13 Jan 1786, d. 11 Sep 1867 at 81y 8m.

W 17   COMPHER, Peter, b. 21 May 1793, d. 3 Mar 1886 at 92y 9m 12d.

W 18   LYNN, Lydia Jane, b. 14 Apr 1845, d. 15 Mar 1905.

W 19   LEWIS, Mary C. E., daughter of Robt. & Caroline LEWIS, d. 19 May 1878 at 28y 8m 24d.

W 20   LEWIS, Anna J., wife of John H. LEWIS, d. 7 Jan 1884 at 25y 6m 4d.

W 21   LEWIS, John H., b. 3 May 1854, d. 17 Nov 1935.

W 22   WILT, Samuel Franklin, son of Daisy E. & J. F. WILT, b. 3 Dec 1908, d. 17 Dec 1913 at 5y 14d.

[first stone is 70 feet from fence]

X 1   WINE, Catherine, wife of Jacob WINE, b. 24 Mar 1755, d. 25 Aug 1826 at 71y 5m 1d.

X 2   SLATER, Michael, son of John SLATER, d. 8 Feb 1826 at 24y 3m 23d.

X 3   SLATER, Jacob, d. 29 Oct 1898 at 59y 1m 14d.

X 4   AULT, Rachel, d. 25 Aug 1834 at 68y 3m 18d.

X 5   FRY, Enos, b. 7 Aug 1842, d. 11 Sep 1852 at 10y 1m 1d.

X 6   COMPHER, Elizabeth Almira, only daughter of Joseph & Susannah COMPHER,
            d. 14 Jun 1865 at 15y 1m 20d.

X 7   WALTMAN, Joseph, b. 11 Feb 1800, d. 21 Jun 1870.

X 8   WALTMAN, Col. Enanuel, b. 6 Dec 1797, d. 2 Dec 1866 at 68y 11m 26d.

X 9   STONEBURNER, Daniel, b. 5 Aug 1796,m d. 12 Apr 1869.

X 10   BARTLETT, Elizabeth H., b. 17 Jun 1835, d. 9 Feb 1872 at 36y 7m 23d.

X 11   WILLIAMS, Henry S., son of Israel, d. 10 May 1872 at 53 yrs.

X 12   STONEBURNER, Sarah, b. May 1808, d. 1 Jun 1875 at 67yrs.

X 13   STONEBURNER, Catharine, b. 5 Sep 1801, d. 16 Sep 1879 at 79y 11d.

X 14   WILLIAMS, Ann M., wife of H. S. WILLIAMS, b. 1 Sep 1821, d. 10 Mar 1889.

Y 1   CEMPHER, John W., infant son of Saml. & H. CEMPHER, d. 26 Jan 1844 at 9d.

Y 2   CRIM, Charles, d. 17 Sep 1824 at 80y 11m 18d.

[110 foot space]

Y 3   — Catherine 1830. [illegible]

Y 4   WIRTS, Margaret, daughter of Peter & Christine WIRTS, d. 24 Mar 1870 at 68 yrs.
            [illegible]

Y 5   SWANK, Alcinda, b. 15 Oct 1822, d. 28 Mar 1871 at 48y 5m 12d.

Y 6   FRY, Mary C., wife of Jacob FRY, b. 19 Feb 1838, d. 18 Aug 1871 at 88y 5m 29d.

Y 7   VIRTS, John A., b. 25 May 1806, d. 9 Nov 1874 at 68y 5m 14d.

Y 8   MILES, Annie I., wife of John W. MILES, b. 4 Jul 1851, d. 8 Feb 1876 at 24y 7m 4d.

Y 9   TALTON, George W., d. 13 Apr 1911 at 42y 1m.

[First stone lower side of hill, 155 feet from fence]

Z 1   SPEAKS, Sytha Ann Vyletter, daughter of Charles C. & Sarah Ann SPEAKS, b. 17 Feb 1851,
            d. 1 Mar 1851 at 12d.

Z 2   COOPER, Elizabeth Jane, daughter of George & Mary C. COOPER, b. 6 Sep 1850,
            d. 9 Apr 1851 at 7m 3d.

Z 3   COOPER, Mary Virginia, daughter of George & Mary Catharine COOPER, b. 1 Nov 1852,
            d. 6 Nov 1852 at 6d.

Z 4   COOPER, Lydia E., daughter of G. & M. C. COOPER, d. 24 Feb 1864 at 8d.

Z 5   COOPER, Clara Esther, daughter of George & Mary C. COOPER, b. 11 Oct 1854,
            d. 3 Sep 1855 at 10m 23d.

[First stone is 80 feet from fence on lower side of hill]

AA 1   WINE, Jacob, b. 6 Oct 1757, d. 11 Oct 1823 at 60y 5d.

AA 2   AXLINE, John, d. 19 Feb 1833 at 93y 5m. [D.A.R. Marker]

AA 3   AXLINE, Christina, wife of John AXLINE, d. 16 Apr 1828 at 78 yrs.

AA 4   POTTERFIELD, Catharine, consort of Samuel POTTERFIELD, b. 25 Dec 1806, d. 16 Aug 1846
              at 39y 7m 21d.

AA 5   VICKERS, Isabel F., daughter of William & Sarah VICKERS, d. 3 Aug 1852 at 4y 2d.

AA 6   WHITEHOUSE, Mary J., b. 27 Feb 1837, d. 1 Jul 1852 at 15y 4m 4d.

AA 7   COOPER, Harry E., son of George & Mary C. COOPER, d. 3 Oct 1880 at 6y 8m 4d.

AA 8   SMITH, Henry T., son of Job & Lydia SMITH, b. 23 Feb 1851, d. 18 Aug 1871 at 20y 5m 25d.

BB 1   GRUBB, John Ebenezer, son of E. L. & Cecilia GRUBB, b. 18 Jan 1855, d. 22 Aug 1855 at 7m 4d.

BB 2   GRUBB, Leah, wife of Ebenezer GRUBB, b. 13 Dec 1800, d. 14 Dec 1869 at 69y 1d.

BB 3   GRUBB, Ebenezer, b. 1 Dec 1792, d. 1 Dec 1874 at 82 yrs.

BB 4   COOPER, Frederick, d. 29 Apr 1825 at 58 yrs.

BB 5   RICKERT, Amila, daughter of George RICKERT, d. 25 Jul 1816 at 7m 3w 4d. [broken]

BB 6   RICKARD, Catharine, wife of George RICKARD, d. 7 Sep 1823 at 28y 23d.

BB 7   HOUSEHOLDER, Adam, b. 12 Feb 1808, d. 14 Sep 1882 at 74y 7m 2d.

BB 8   HOUSEHOLDER, Daniel, b. 15 Mar 1774, d. 17 Nov 1865 at 91y 8m 2d.

BB 9   HOUSEHOLDER, Catharine, wife of Daniel HOUSEHOLDER, b. 12 Apr 1776,
              d. 21 Jun 1820.

BB 10   HECKMAN, Rachel, wife of Peter HECKMAN, d. 2 Sep 1816 at 32y 4m 3d.

BB 11   HOUSEHOLDER, Susanna Shafer, wife of Adam HOUSEHOLDER, d. 2 Sep 1819 at 61 yrs.

BB 12   SHAFFER, John, d. 13 Jan 1828 at 27y 10m 16d.

BB 13   ILLEGIBLE - fieldstone

BB 14   GOODHART, John H. Clay, son of Lawrence W. & Sophia GOODHART, d. 29 Oct 1847 at
              2y 2m 1d.

BB 15   GOODHART , Sarah J. M., b. 13 Oct 1849, d. 26 Feb 1850.

BB 15   GOODHART, George E., d. 25 Jul 1854 at 15d.

BB 15   GOODHART, John H. C., b. 8 Jul 1815, d. 29 Oct 1847.

BB 16   VIRTS, William, b. 4 Dec 1771, d. 9 Dec 1853 at 82y 5d.

BB 17   SPRING, Casper, b. 16 Apr 1788, d. 4 Jan 1868 at 79y 8m 19d.

BB 18 SPRING, Elizabeth, wife of Casper SPRING, d. 6 Sep 1883 at 91y 11m 3d.

BB 19 MANN, Mary E., daughter of C. & J. MANN, d. 27 Jan 1874 at 2m 26d.

BB 20 VINCIL, Ginettie, b. 27 Aug 1848, d. 8 Mar 1871 at 22y 6m 11d.

BB 21 WRIGHT, Lizzie Chilettie, daughter of Samuel F. & Margaret H. A. WRIGHT,
           d. 30 Oct 1881 at 6y 9m 9d.

CC 1   ROLLER, Conrad, d. 8 Oct 1824 at 72y 7m 1w 5d.

CC 2   ROLLER, Elizabeth, d. 22 Feb 1845 at 83y 2m 11d.

CC 3   BOGER, Michael, b. 1 Apr 1762, d. 26 Mar 1822 at 59y 11m 1d.

CC 4   BOGER, Mary Elizabeth, b. 27 Jul 1761, d. 13 Dec 1813 at 79y 1m 17d.

CC 5   SMITH, Susannah, wife of T. SMITH, d. 7 Mar 1826 at 82y 4m 1d. [illegible]

CC 6   C. E. A. [field stone]

[space of 50 feet]

CC 7   GOODHART, Lydia E., daughter of J. W. & S. W. GOODHART, b. 30 Aug 1856,
           d. 20 Dec 1868.

CC 8   GOODHART, Mary S., daughter of J. W. & S. W. GOODHART, b. 24 Feb 1851,
           d. 13 Nov 1863.

CC 9   GOODHART, Sophia W., wife of J. W. GOODHART, b. 15 May 1817, d. 27 Feb 1871 at
           29y 8m 2d.

CC 10 COOPER, Annie E., b. 30 Mar 1843, d. 2 Dec 1872 at 29y 8m 2d.

[space of 30 feet]

CC 11 SWANK, Peter, son of Philip & Mary SWANK, b. 6 Jan 1826, d. 27 May 1847.

CC 12 COMPHER, Cora V., daughter of William F. & Sarah C. COMPHER, b. 31 May 1873,
           d. 15 Sep 1874 at 1y 3m 15d.

CC 13 MANN, Rosetta May, d. 2 Mar 1891 at 10m 7d.

CC 14 TRITAPOE, Laura Millannette, daughter of Samuel & Sarah F. TRITAPOE, b. 20 Feb 1870,
           d. 9 Jun 1875 at 5y 3m 18d.

CC 15 COMPHER, Dasie N., daughter of F. & J. COMPHER, b. 22 Jan 1875.

CC 16 VICKERS, Rachel A. C., wife of John T. VICKERS, b. 9 Sep 1846, d. 22 Feb 1896 [stone lists
           children: Allice, John G. , Thomas H., Ellen C., Charles, Eunice L., Edward F.,
           James H., Mary G., Susannah, Samuel, and William].

CC 17   WADE, Ellenor, d. 5 Oct 1900 at 83yrs.

CC 18   VICKERS, John T., b. 12 Jan 1845, d. 29 Mar 1910.

[First stone is 160 feet from fence on lower side of hill]

DD 1   WIRTS, Sarah P., daughter of Peter & Christine WIRTS, d. 28 Apr 1876 at 63yrs.

DD 2   SMITH, John A., b. 1 Mar 1851, d. 10 Aug 1870 at 19y 5m 9d.

DD 3   FRY, George W., b. 12 Apr 1838, d. 19 Feb 1872 at 33y 10m 7d.

DD 4   FRY, Martha E., wife of George W. FRY, b. 7 Apr 1842, d. 24 Sep 1874 at 32y 5m 17d.

DD 5   ROLLER, Rachel, b. 1 Nov 1799, d. 25 Mar 1872 at 72y 4m 21d.

DD 6   ROLLER, Frederick, b. 17 Jan 1799, d. 20 Jan 1875 at 85y 3d.

DD 7   JACOBS, Nellie B., daughter of John & Mary JACOBS, d. 6 Sep 1892 at 8y 5m 22d.

EE 1   ROLLER, Christian, son of Conrad ROLLER, d. 18 Jun 1797 at 2y 7m.

EE 2   ROLLER, Samuel, son of Conrad ROLLER, d. 8 Oct 1805 at 1yr.

EE 3   SMITH, William, d. 26 Mar 1808 at 22y 9m.

EE 4   MILLER, Michael, d. Sep 1806 at 35y a few days.

EE 5   FRY, Polly, wife of John FRY, b. 20 May 1799, d. 24 Jun 1821 at 23y 26d.

EE 6   ILLEGIBLE

EE 7   HUNT, Jacob, 1806 [broken fieldstone]

EE 8   SHUMAKER, Jonathan, b. 2 Feb 1816, 14 Sep 1863 at 47y 6m 14d.

EE 9   SHUMAKER, Simon, b. 1 Oct 1784, d. 10 Apr 1857 at 72y 6m 9d.

EE 10   MORRISON, Hannah Ann, daughter of Archibald & Rachel MORRISON, d. 16 Jul 1851
          at 14d.

EE 11   MORRISON, George Henry Clay, son of Archibald & Marry M. MORRISON, d. 15 Sep 1854
          at 1y 2m 28d.

EE 12   MORRISON, Sophia E., daughter of Archibald & Rachel MORRISON, d. 15 Sep 1854 at
          11y 5m 1d.

EE 13   MORRISON, Rachel, wife of Archibald MORRISON, b. 8 Aug 1818, d. 24 Jan 1852 at
          33y 5m 16d.

EE 14   SWANK, Mary, wife of Philip SWANK, b. 23 Sep 1786, d. 15 May 1839.

EE 15   WORDSWORTH, Mary F., daughter of Lewis & Catherine WORDSWORTH,
          d. 23 Aug 1850 at 9m 28d.

EE 16   WIARD, Mary, wife of Michael WIARD, d. 18 May 1869 at 65y 1m 15d.

EE 17   WIARD, Michael, 22 Dec 1889 at 92y 7m 9d.

EE 18   FRY, Sarah, d. 3 Dec 1866 at 61y 1m 28d.

EE 19   FRY, Robert W., d. 21 Mar 1890 at 7m 4d.

EE 20   VICKERS, Samuel, son of J. T. & Rachel VICKERS, b. 10 Dec 1889, d. 10 Apr 1891 at 1y 4m.

[first stone is 20 feet from fence]

FF 1   SLATER, John, d. 15 Jan 1824 at 60y 2m 22d.

FF 2   SLATER, Catherine, wife of John SLATER, d. 6 Sep 1807 at 35yrs.

FF 3   STONEBURNER, Adam, d. 11 Jan 1826 at 31y 4m 21d.

FF 4   BAKER, Elizabeth, daughter of William BAKER, d. 17 Apr 1808 at 10m 6d.

FF 5   VIRTS, Elizabeth, wife of Michael VIRTS, b. 19 Jun 1816, d. 5 Oct 1857 at 41y 3m 16d.

FF 6   VIRTS, Michael, b. 2 Jun 1797, d. 4 Sep 1851 at 54y 2m 2d.

FF 7   SCHWANK, Catharine, b. 10 Sep 1776, d. 11 Dec 1850 at 74y 3m 1d.

FF 8   –RY, Margaret, consort of [broken]

FF 9   FRY, Philip, d. 2 Oct 1839 at 73y 2m. [illegible]

FF 10   FRY, Sarah Ann, daughter of William FRY, b. 30 Aug 1837, d. 9 Apr 1850 at 12y 7m 10d.

FF 11   ROLER, Conrad, b. 7 Feb 1786, d. 11 Aug 1852 at 66y 6m 7d.

FF 12   YAKEY, Anna M., 6 Mar 1786, d. 15 Jan 1870.

FF 13   COOPER, Henry C., d. 19 Dec 1888 at 56y 2m 25d.

FF 14   COOPER, George F., d. 19 Aug 1894 at 63y 10m 6d.

FF 15   COOPER, Sarah J., d. 16 Sep 1914 at 82 yrs.

GG 1   COOPPER, Adam, son of Phillip COOPPER, 4 Sep – [illegible]

GG 2   SCHMIDT, Jacob, d. 21 Feb 1796 [German inscription]

GG 3   MAN, Leanah, wife of John MAN, daughter of Philip EVERHART, b. 28 Jan 1806, d. 31 Dec 1824 at 18y 11m 3d.

GG 4   MANN, Louisa Ann, daughter of John & Anna Mary MANN, d. 25 Jun 1817 at 5y 3m 13d.

GG 5   MOORE, Elenor I., daughter of John & Mary E. MOORE, d. 22 Jan 1825 at 11m 19d.

GG 6   STONEBURNER, John Leonitus, d. 18 Oct 1825 at 2y 1m.

GG 7   AUMENT, George, son of Lawrence AUMENT, b. 1788, d. 24 Apr 1819 at 31y 8m 4d.

GG 8   AUMENT, Lawrence, husband of Barbara, d. 13 Feb 1814 at 50y 3w 3d.

GG 9   AUMENT, Moley, wife of Antney AUMAN, d. 16 Dec 1806 at 40y 1m 1d.

GG 10   AUMEN, Rebecca, daughter of Lawrence AUMEN, d. 22 Mar 1826 at 23y 11m 11d.

[first stone is 15 feet from fence]

HH 1   AXLINE, George, son of Jacob AXLINE, d. 16 Jun 1803 at 1y 1d.

HH 2   COOPER, Ann Catharine [no date] at 21y 2m 5d.

HH 3   COOPPER, Michael, Sr., b. 20 Jun 1742, d. 19 Feb 1815 at 72y 7m 3w 6d.

HH 4   COMPHER, John, Sr., b. 16 Oct 1740, d. 26 Mar 1815 at 75y 5m 10d.

HH 5   COMPHER, Maria Cathren, wife of John COMPHER, Sr., b. 4 Feb 1755, d. 14 Mar 1815 at
              60 yrs.

HH 6   COMPHER, Peter, b. 24 Aug 1776, d. 5 Nov 1858 at 82y 2m 12d.

HH 7   COMPHER, Susanna, wife of Peter COMPHER, b. 12 Mar 1779, d. 5 Apr 1815 at 36y 3w 3d.

[Curved row begins 15 feet from fence]

II 1   WIRTZ, William, b. 23 Dec 1792, d. 29 Sep 1878 at 85y 9m 6d.

II 2   WIZES, Catherine, d. 10 Aug 1804 at 36y 4m.

II 2   WIZES, infant at 10m.

II 2   WIZES, Mical at 44yrs.

II 3   ILLEGIBLE - [fieldstone]

II 4   BOGER, Frederick, b. 7 Feb 1752, d. 16 Oct 1791 at 39y 2m 2w 4d. [illegible]

II 5   EVERHART, Lydia, wife of Joseph EVERHART, d. 13 Apr 1830 at 24y 8m 15d.

II 6   WALTMAN, Jacob; Margaret, his wife; Elizabeth, his second wife; Elias, his son died
              12 May 1827 at 24 yrs. [Elias' death date]

II 7   WALTMAN, Emanuel, son of Jacob WALTMAN, Sr., d. 24 Jan 1821 at 15y 9m.

II 8   WALMAN, Sara, daughter of John WALMAN, d. 10 Mar 1816 at 9m 2w.

II 9   WALTMAN, Jacob, Sr., d. 8 Oct 1823 at 78 yrs.

II 10   WALTMAN, Margaret H., wife of Jacob WALTMAN, Sr., d. 15 Jan 1809 at 65 yrs.

II 11   WALTMAN, Margaret, wife of Jacob WALTMAN, d. 30 Jan 1807 at 30y 11m 10d.

II 12   FAWLEY, John, d. 11 Jun 1803 at 83y 5m 11d.

II 13   FAWLEY, Anna Maria, wife of John FAWLEY, d. 2 Oct 1803 at 66 yrs.

II 14   AMRY, John, son of Jacob AMRY, d. 27 Jun 1803 at 20y 7m 13d.

II 15   AMRY, Adam, son of Jacob AMRY, Dec'd, d. 26 Jun 1813 at 28y 2w.

II 16   EMERY, Catharine, wife of Jacob EMERY, d. 27 Mar 1834 at about 72 yrs.

II 17   EMERY, Jacob, d. 29 Oct 1815 at 71y 9m.

II 18   SHEWMAKER, Leah, daughter of Simon & Catharine SHEWMAKER, b. 26 Dec 1830,
           d. 16 Aug 1832.

II 19   SHUMAKER, Catharine, wife of Simon SHUMAKER, b. 18 Sep 1790, d. 23 Feb 1857 at
           66y 5m 5d.

[First stone is 175 feet from fence on lower side of hill]

JJ 1   CARNES, Silas C., son of Samuel L. & Sarah M. CARNES, b. 28 May 1854, d. 17 Nov 1866 at
           11y 11m 20d.

JJ 2   FRY, John A. N., son of George & Margaret FRY, b. 6 Aug 1865, d. 22 Mar 1867 at 1y 5m 16d.

JJ 3   JACOBS, Sarah F. E., daughter of James W. & Catharine H. JACOBS, d. 4 Aug 1867 at
           5m 14d.

JJ 4   BRAMHALL, Robert, b. 26 Nov 1871, d. 8 Jan 1906.

[Curved row begins 15 feet from fence]

KK 1   VIRTZS, Peter, son of John VIRTZS, d. 23 Apr 1812 at 35y 2m 1w 2d.

KK 2   VIRTZS, Christine, wife of Peter VIRTZS, d. 20 Jun 1813 at 76y 5m 3w 2d.

KK 3   WIZE, Peter, d. 22 May 1798 at 60y 1m 9d.

KK 4   WIRZ, Willem, d. 1782 [fieldstone]

KK 5   FRYE, Dorethy, wife of Philip FRYE, d. 31 Aug 1827 at 96y 2w 18d [this May be 69 years].

KK 6   FRY, Philip, d. 11 Aug 1831 at 88 yrs.

KK 7   EVERHART, Mortimer, son of Jacob EVERHART, d. 11 May 1826 at 3m 18d.

KK 8   EVERHART, Ann Elizabeth, daughter of Jacob & Sarah EVERHART, d. 6 Jan 1830 at
           2y 1d. [broken]

KK 9   EVERHART, Jacob, b. 3 Feb 1796, d. 23 Nov 1828.

KK 10   WALTMAN, Georg Freiedrich Emanuel, d. 1800 at 38y 11m. [German inscription]

KK 10   WALTMAN, William, son of John WALTMAN, d. 23 May 1813.

KK 11   WALTMAN, Imanuel, d. 13 Feb 1784 at 69 yrs.

KK 12   WALTMAN, Margaret, wife of Imanuel, d. 13 Oct 1786 at 57yrs.

KK 13   WALTMAN, Margaret, daughter of Jacob WALTMAN, d. Jan 1789 at 17y 6m 8d.

KK 14   HOUSHOLTER, Catharine, wife of Adam HOUSHOLTER, d. 10 Sep 1794 at 44 yrs.

KK 15   HOUSHOLTER, Adam, d. 27 Sep 1804 at 55 yrs.

KK 16   HUF, Philip, d. 9 Mar 1796 at 33y 3m.

KK 17   C. M. F. 1803.

KK 18   STOUTSENBERGER, Mary, wife of Samuel STOUTSENBERGER, b. 11 May 1826,
                d. 8 Sep 1854 at 28yrs.

KK 19   STOUTSENBERGER, Samuel, b. 13 Dec 1801, d. 13 Mar 1847 at 45y 3m.

KK 20   STOUTSENBERGER, Mary, consort of Samuel STOUTSENBERGER, b. 11 Apr 1801,
                d. 11 Jun 1842 at 41y 2m.

KK 21   STATLER, Priscilla, d. 28 Feb 1852 at 85 yrs.

KK 22   STATLER, John, d. 30 Jun 1856 at 97 yrs.

KK 23   SWANK, Philip, b. 10 Jan 1782, d. 8 Aug 1854 at 72y 6m 29d.

KK 24   COMPHER, Hannah, wife of Samuel COMPHER, daughter of Israel & Amelia WILLIAMS,
                b. 1 Dec 1817, d. 1 Sep 1868 at 38 y 9m.

KK 25   COMPHER, Milly Ann, daughter of Samuel & Hannah COMPHER, b. 15 Mar 1842,
                d. 10 Mar 1867 at 24y 11m 25d.

KK 26   FRY, Sarah C. E., wife of Daniel J. H. FRY, daughter of Samuel & Hannah COMPHER,
                b. 16 Sep 1840, d. 19 Sep 1867 at 27y 3d.

KK 27   COMPHER, Samuel, b. 8 Oct 1818, d. 26 Mar 1883.

KK 28   COMPHER, Ulysses S., son of Jonas J. & Mary C. COMPHER, b. 18 Oct 1866, d. 18 Aug 1868 at
                1y 9m 21d.

[First stone is 120 feet from fence on lower side of hill]

LL 1   FAWLEY, Henry Washington, son of Joseph & Catherine FAWLEY, b. 17 Jan 1849,
                d. 11 Jul 1851 at 2y 5m 24d.

LL 2   CORDELL, Susan, wife of Adam CORDELL, daughter of Jacob & Catharine SLATER,
                b. 27 May 1809, d. 18 Jun 1853 at 44y 22d.

LL 3   LYNN, Nicholas, b. 21 Nov 1804, d. 18 Jul 1866 at 61y 7m 27d.

LL 4   LYNN, Elizabeth, b. 11 Oct 1805, d. 8 Mar 1867 at 61y 4m 27d.

LL 5   JACOBS , Sarah, wife of Bynard JACOBS, b. 25 Mar 1813, d. 19 Apr 1881 at 68y 24d.

LL 6   McDONOUGH, Bettie, daughter of L. H. & E. A. McDONOUGH, b. 17 Sep 1866,
                d. 15 Aug 1868.

LL 6   McDONOUGH, Willie, son of L. H. & E. A. McDONOUGH, b. 4 Aug 1864, d. 9 May 1870.

LL 7   PARSON, Hector, infant of T. M. & S. J. PARSON, b. 28 Jan 1870, d. 10 Jul 1870
                at 5m 12d. [broken]

LL 8   JACOBS, James W., d. 15 Jan 1902 at 59y 9m 7d.

LL 9   BRAMHALL, Blanco W., b. 29 Feb 1828, d. 26 May 1903.

LL 10   BRAMHALL, Rebecca J., b. 7 Oct 1836, d. 11 Nov 1910.

[First stone lower side of hill, 180 feet from fence]

MM 1   ARNOLD, Estella V., daughter of Noah & Emeline ARNOLD, b. 14 Aug 1843, d. 18 Oct 1865
            at 22 yrs.

MM 2   CRUMBAKER, Elizabeth, daughter of Solomon & Catharine CRUMBAKER, b. 10 Jul 1813,
            d. 10 Oct 1870.

MM 3   CRUMBAKER, Solomon, b. 25 Jul 1784, d. 8 Jan 1866 at 81y 5m 13d.

MM 4   CRUMBAKER, Annie C., b. 22 Aug 1787, d. 9 Oct 1866 at 79y 1m 17d.

MM 5   AXLINE, John W., son of David E. & Martha AXLINE [no dates]

MM 6   UNKNOWN - Sunken stone

[First stone is 60 feet from fence on lower side of hill]

NN 1   RUSE, Christian, d. 20 Sep 1821 at 75 yrs. [illegible - fieldstone]

NN 2   RUSE, Catharine, d. 15 Aug 1802 at 35 yrs.

NN 3   RUSE, Elizabeth, d. 1807 at –y 8m 3w. [illegible]

NN 4   JOUER, John, b. 19 Feb 1788, d. 19 Feb 1826.

NN 5   CORDELL, America Virginia, daughter of John & Sarah Ann CORDELL, b. 13 Aug 1851,
            d. 2 Apr 1855 at 7m 19d.

NN 6   –W C– [fieldstone]

NN 7   CRIM, Rosanah, wife of Abraham CRIM, b. 21 Feb 1780, d. 8 Oct 1865 at 85y 7m 15d.

NN 8   HUNTER, Margaret, wife of Michael L. HUNTER, b. 19 Aug 1838, d. 17 Sep 1865 at 27y 29d.

NN 9   HUNTER, Ida C., daughter of M. L. & Margaret HUNTER, d. 6 Feb 1866 at 1y 3m 12d.

NN 10   HUNTER, Walter, son of M. L. & R. H. HUNTER, b. 19 Jun 1873, d. 7 Oct 1873.

NN 11   RUSE, Mary A., daughter of Henry & Sarah RUSE, d. 16 Mar 1865 at 28y 4m 26d.

NN 12   COOPER, Elizabeth, daughter of John & Eve Ann COOPER, b. 9 Nov 1811, d. 9 Jun 1865 at
            53y 7m.

NN 13   CARNES, Marietta, wife of Abram E. CARNES, d. 7 Sep 1865 at 24y 8m 27d.

NN 14   HUNTER, Michael L., b. 12 Jul 1834, d. 3 Jun 1876 at 41y 10m 12d.

NN 15   HUNTER, George P., b. 7 Sep 1831, d. 4 Apr 1907 at 75y 6m 27d.

NN 16   HUNTER, Amanda C., wife of George P. HUNTER, b. 22 Jan 1827, d. 8 Oct 1895 at
            68y 9m 16d.

[Scattered stones in back corner of cemetery]

OO 1   VCKENS, Isack L. - 1770 [fieldstone]

OO 2   STONEBURNER, Juliana, wife of Frederick STONEBURNER, b. 20 Mar 1762, d. 28 Feb 1799
                at 36y 11m.

OO 3   DAVIS, Esther, b. – Aug 1750, d. 16 Sep 1795 at 45y 1m.

OO 4   ROLLER, John, d. 26 Sep 1802 at 71y 10m 5d.

OO 5   SMITH, Jacob, 13 Apr 1805 at 61y 11m.

OO 6   VIRTZ, Barbary E., d. 1790 at 57 yrs.

[First stone is 135 feet from fence]

PP 1   VIRTS, Lucy Ann, daughter of Peter & Leah VIRTS, b. 17 May 1838, d. 28 Aug 1864 at
                26y 3m 11d.

PP 2   BEST, Albert, b. 7 Jan 1807, d. 22 Feb 1864 at 57y 1m 15d.

PP 3   KERN, Margaret, d. 24 Mar 1864 at 58y 10m 19d.

PP 4   VIRTS, William H., son of Peter & Leah VIRTS, b. 28 Dec 1842, d. 8 Aug 1867.

PP 5   MANN, Elizabeth, wife of Joseph MANN, b. 28 Nov 1807, d. 5 Apr 1879.

PP 6   MANN, Joseph, b. 12 Oct 1804, d. 12 Jul 1864 at 59y 9m.

PP 7   SPRING, John, d. Oct 1865 at 65 yrs.

PP 8   RUSE, Michael, d. 26 Oct 1864 at 78y 8m 8d. [broken]

PP 9   RUSE, Sallie, wife of Henry RUSE, d. 19 Nov 1894 at 91y 10m 6d.

PP 10   RUSE, Henry, d. 2 Feb 1865 at 71y 4m 8d.

PP 11   BEST, Elizabeth, d. 18 Mar 1894 at 84y 2m 14d.

[First stone is 140 feet from fence]

QQ 1   WIRTS, Peter, b. 9 Dec 1812, d. 1 Nov 1868 at 55y 10m 22d.

QQ 2   ALDER, Albert, b. 4 Apr 1811, d. 22 Feb 1864 at 49y 10m 18d.

QQ 3   FRY, Mary Catherine, wife of John D. FRY, d. 24 Mar 1864 at 30y 11m 18d.

QQ 4   EVERHART, William F., b. 3 Jul 1844, d. 10 Aug 1864 at 20y 1m 7d.

QQ 5   LUCKETT, Virginia C., eldest daughter of Samuel C. & Mary B. LUCKETT, d. 23 Aug 1864
                at 25 yrs.

QQ 6   LUCKETT, Samuel C., youngest son of Samuel C. & Mary B. LUCKETT, d. 28 Feb 1867 at
                15 yrs.

QQ 7   WHITE, Crawford K., d. 3 Dec 1865 at 38 yrs.

[First stone is 115 feet from fence]

RR 1   STONE, Samuel S., d. 13 Mar 1880 at 69y 18d.

RR 2   STONE, Edgar H., b. 4 Dec 1852, d. 14 Jan 1877 at 24y 1m 10d.

RR 3   STONE, Eleanor W., daughter of Samuel & Elizabeth STONE, d. 26 Jun 1865 at 18y 3m 26d.

RR 4   STONE, Thomas M., son of Samuel & Elizabeth STONE, d. 19 Apr 1865 at 24y 9m 9d.

RR 5   STONE, Samuel F., son of Samuel & Elizabeth STONE, b. 30 Sep 1844, d. 30 Oct 1863 at
                19y 1m.

RR 6   HICKMAN, John, b. 6 Dec 1816, d. 19 Nov 1863 at 46y 11m 3d.

RR 7   POTTERFIELD, Samuel, b. 1 Mar 1799, d. 17 Nov 1863 at 64y 8m 16d.

RR 8   COOPER, John, son of George & Mary COOPER, b. 1 Aug 1797, d. 12 Dec 1863 at 66y 4m 11d.

RR 9   HICKMAN, William, b. 19 Oct 1814, d. 9 Jan 1864 at 49y 2m 20d.

RR 10   SPRING, George F., d. 13 Feb 1864 at 18y 5m 12d.

RR 11   COMPHER, Ebenezer N., son of John & Elizabeth M. COMPHER, d. 4 Nov 1863 at 7y 15d.

RR 12   FRY, Daniel C. S., son of Noah & S. FRY, d. 2 May 1864 at 10y 2m 11d.

RR 13   LEWIS, Mitta M. F., daughter of Robert & Caroline A. LEWIS, b. 6 May 1863, d. 18 Oct 1864
                at 1y 5m.

RR 14   SHAFER, Harry, infant son of John H. & Emma C. SHAFER, d. 22 Jan 1864.

RR 15   COMPHER, Charles C., son of John H. & Margaret A. COMPHER, b. 16 Oct 1864,
                d. 10 Jul 1865 at 8m 24d.

RR 16   BOWERS, John H., b. 13 Dec 1820, d. 23 Feb 1880 at 59y 2m 10d.

[First stone is 115 feet from fence]

SS 1   MANN, Mary E, daughter of Jacob & Ann MANN, b. 6 Oct 1851, d. 17 Jun 1863 at 11y 8m 11d.

SS 1   MANN, Virginia E., daughter of Jacob & Ann MANN, b. 30 Jan 1854, d. 30 Jun 1863 at 9y 5m

SS 2   BOWERS, Mary A., wife of John H. BOWERS, b. 24 Aug 1823, d. 3 Jan 1868.

[First stone is 90 feet from fence]

TT 1   DOWNEY, Calvin Welty, d. 26 Mar 1885 at 30y 11m 22d.

TT 2   DOWNEY, J. M., b. 12 Dec 1809, d. 28 Mar 1881 at 71y 3m 16d.

TT 3   DOWNEY, Annie E., b. 3 Jun 1812, d. 16 Mar 1881 at 68y 11m 13d.

TT 4   DOWNEY, W. Scott, d. 12 Feb 1878 at 30y 9m 1d.

TT 5   DOWNEY, William Burns, d. 9 Mar 1873 at 37 yrs.

TT 6   DOWNEY, John F., son of J. M. & A. E. DOWNEY, d. 1 Apr 1862 at 23 yrs. in the service of
           country.

TT 7   DOWNEY, Rose J., daughter of J. M. & A. E. DOWNEY, 7 Aug 1867 at 17 yrs.

TT 8   DOWNEY, Leila B., daughter of J. M. & A. E. DOWNEY, 2 Jan 1865 at 17 yrs.

TT 9   DOWNEY, Amanda K., daughter of J. M. & A. E. DOWNEY, 13 Jan 1861 at 24 yrs.

TT 10   WEBSTER, Alice S., daughter of J. M. & A. E. DOWNEY, 1 Aug 1863 at 22 yrs.

TT 11   MYERS, Peter C., b. 30 Sep 1813, d. 23 Aug 1863 at 49y 10m 23d.

TT 12   HAMILTON, James W., b. 18 Dec 1820, d. 8 Oct 1863.

TT 13   HAMILTON, Lydia, daughter of James & Caroline HAMILTON, b. 5 Nov 1850,
           d. 12 Sep 1881.

TT 14   HUNTER, William, b. 11 Mar 1798, d. 21 Jul 1863 at 65y 4m 9d.

TT 15   VINCEL, Delilah, wife of Luther H. VINCEL, b. 20 Dec 1838, d. 30 Oct 1863 at 24 yrs.

TT 16   SPRING, Lillie C., daughter of Charles W. & Laura J. SPRING, d. 14 May 1875 at 5m 1d.

TT 17   HUNTER, Sevila, wife of William HUNTER, b. 13 Jul 1795, d. 25 Feb 1862 at 66y 7m 12d.

[First stone is 110 feet from fence]

UU 1   COMPHER, Susan, b. 25 Sep 1810, d. 23 Oct 1879 at 69y 28d.

UU 2   BRAMHALL, Walter E., son of Blanco W. & R. J. BRAMHALL, b. 10 Sep 1864, d. 9 Aug 1865
           at 10m 30d.

UU 3   BOGER, Sarah C., daughter of S. & M. BOGER, d. 13 Oct 1878 at 12y 11m.

UU 4   BOGER, James, b. 10 Feb 1799, d. 24 Jun 1871.

UU 5   BOGER, Mary E., daughter of Jacob & Mary BOGER, b. 20 Oct 1869, d. 9 Mar 1870.

UU 6   BOGER, Philip, d. 16 Jun 1865 at 76y 11m 1d.

UU 7   BOGER, Mary A., d. 14 Dec 1876 at 60y 9m.

UU 8   BOGER, Samuel L., b. 5 Feb 1806, d. 30 Jun 1867 at 61y 4m 25d.

UU 9   SIMONS, Henry M., son of Edward & Mary A. SIMONS, d. 10 Aug 1863 at 19y 1m 25d.

UU 10   SIMONS, William E. F. J., son of Edward & Mary Ann SIMONS, b. 30 Oct 1855,
           d. 7 Mar 1859 at 3y 4m 8d.

UU 11   BOGER, John, b. 24 Sep 1801, d. 29 Jan 1862.

UU 12   ALDER, Sarah C., consort of George W. ALDER, b. 12 Mar 1834, d. 13 Aug 1862 at 28y 5m.

UU 13   ALDER, Wm. R., son of George W. & Sarah ALDER, b. 30 Mar 1862, d. 22 Oct 1862.

UU 14   KABRICK, Peter J., b. 28 Apr 1831, d. 21 Sep 1862.

UU 15   COMPHER, John, b. 11 Apr 1806, d. 12 Oct 1862 at 59y 6m 1d.

UU 16   COOPER, Lydia E., wife of William F. COOPER, d. 29 Dec 1862 at 35yrs.

UU 17   COOPER, Joseph, son of William F. & Lydia E. COOPER, 27 May 1856, d. 25 Aug 1863.

UU 18   COOPER, William F., son of William F. & Lydia E. COOPER, b. 23 Sep 1854, d. 11 Sep 1863.

UU 19   FAWLEY, Sally Ann, daughter of John & Mary FAWLEY, b. 12 Oct 1858, d. 10 Dec 1862 at
              4y 1m 29d.

[Stones are located along the back fence]

Pile   BOGER, Peter, d. 19 Feb 1790 [Broken - German inscription]

Pile   CRIM, John H., b. 12 Feb 1816, d. 5 Oct 1879 at 63 yrs.

Pile   FRY, Mary E., daughter of Joseph & S. E. FRY, d. 12 Jul 1865 at 8m 12d.

Pile   JACOBS, John S., d. 23 Dec 1864 at 37 yrs.

Pile   RICHARDSON, Virginia C., daughter of Rev. X. J. RICHARDSON, d. 28 Jun 1868 at
              12y 9m 17d.

Pile   ROFF, Johannes, d. 1794 at 43y 2m 3w [German inscription]

Pile   ROLLER, Rosena, wife of John ROLLER, d. 30 Feb 1794 at 69y 3m.

Pile   SCHAEFFER, Elizabeth, d. 9 Jan 1897 at 90y 10m 1d.

Pile   SCHMIT, H. L. John, d. 21 Oct 1793.

Pile   WALTMAN, Jacob, b. 6 Nov 1793, d. 21 Apr 1865 at 71y 5m 15d.

Pile   WILLIAMS, F. P., son of H. S. & M. A. WILLIAMS, b. 7 Jul 1853, d. 4 Oct 1876 at 23y 2m 27d.

Pile   I. G. S. 1785.

[Stones not found in 1994]

List   BROOKS, Iva, d. 17 Oct 1936 at 19 yrs.

List   COMPHER, Jessie W., daughter of John & Elizabeth M. COMPHER, d. 16 Jan 1861 at
              4y 8m 28d.

List   DAVIS, George, son of Jacob & Susan DAVIS, b. 6 Oct 1810, d. 28 Oct 1821 at 11y 22d.

List   ENGLISH, Archibald, son of William T. & L. Maud ENGLISH, b. 21 Sep 1865, d. 15 Dec 1865
              at 2m 26d.

List   FAWLEY, Florence May, daughter of Joseph & Ann C. FAWLEY, b. 2 May 1853, d. 2 Sep 1856
              at 3y 4m.

List   FRY, Mary E., daughter of Joseph H. & S. E. FRY, d. 18 Mar 1864 at 8m 12d.

List   FRY, Ulysses W., son of Joseph H. & S. E. FRY, d. 18 Mar 1867 at 5m 29d.

List   FRYE, Addie Leslie, d. 12 Nov 1942 at 31y 5m 12d.

List   FRYE, Charles Clayton, d. 16 Nov 1942 at 23y 9d.

List   GRUBB, Jacob Curtis, son of E. L. & Cecilia GRUBB, b. 28 Jun 1821, d. 17 Oct 1824 at
                    3y 3m 19d.

List   HICKMAN, Sarah S., d. 10 Feb 1834 at 31y 10m 28d.

List   JACOBS, Chester R., son of John & Mary JACOBS, d. 14 Sep 1892 at 8m.

List   KALB, Margarett Susan, daughter of John G. R. & Ellen M. KALB, d. 6 Apr 1861 at 11y 9d.

List   LANN, James W., 12 Nov 1932 at 68 yrs.

List   MANN, Catharine, infant daughter of William & Margaret MANN, d. 1851.

List   MANN, Lewis W., son of Joseph & Elizabeth MANN, b. 27 Jul 1830, d. 23 Aug 1867 at 37 yrs.

List   MANN, Martin L., son of John & Charity MANN, b. 21 Sep 1860, d. 17 Mar 1861.

List   MANN, Mary C., daughter of John & Charity MANN, 25 Sep 1859, d. 19 Jul 1860.

List   RICHARDS, Samuel D., b. 18 Jul 1823, d. 12 Sep 1836.

List   SHAEFER, Michael, d. 5 Mar 1839 at 25y 15d.

List   SHAFFER, Michael, Sr., d. 30 Jan 1829 at 59y 7m 1d.

List   SPINKS, Cornell F., d. 21 Apr 1941 at 55y 7d.

List   SPINKS, Elizabeth V., d. 2 Jul 1935 at 80y 4m 18d.

List   STONE, Michael, son of Frederick STONE, b. 2 May 1762, d. 28 Feb 1835.

List   STONEBURNER, George, d. 11 Jan 1826 at 31y 4m 21d.

List   VIRTS, Anna E., b. 7 Jul 1851, d. 24 Oct 1906.

List   VIRTS, Mary Ann, wife of Peter VIRTS, b. 5 Nov –, d.   Feb –.

List   WALTMAN, John.

List   WALTMAN, Martha, wife of W. WALTMAN, 13 Oct 1806 [no other date]

List   WRIGHT, Daisy, daughter of S. J. & A. S. WRIGHT, d. 11 Jan 1883.

INDEX

[Entries refer to row and
headstone numbers found in the
Row Listing and not to page
numbers. They refer to the
other people on the headstones,
not the decedent.]

HUNTER Michael L 21
    Michael L. NN 8 R. H.
    NN 10 William TT 17
JACOBS Bynard LL 5
    Catharine H. JJ 3
    Catharine L 16 L 17
    James W. JJ 3 John DD 7
    List Mary DD 7 *List*
    William H. L 16 L 17
JOHNSON Henry A. K 18
KADEL Peter H 5
KALB Ellen M. *List* Ellen M.
    S 18 John G. R. *List*, S 18
    L. A. U 4 S. A. U 4
LEWIS Caroline W 19
    Caroline A. RR 13
    Caroline M. L 20
    Charles M. K 19
    Elizabeth K 19 John H.
    W 20 Robert A. L 20
    Robert RR 13, W 19
LUCKETT Mary B. J 1, QQ 5,
    QQ 6 Samuel C. J 1, K 10,
    QQ 5, QQ 6
MAN John GG 3
MANN Ann SS 1 Anna Mary
    GG 4 C. BB 19 Charity
    List (2) E. S. W 1 Edward
    H 10 Elizabeth K 16, *List*,
    N 12 George G 7 J. BB 19
    J. W. W 1 Jacob SS 1 John
    G 6, GG 4, L 2, *List* (2),
    P 14 Joseph K 16 *List*
    N 12, PP 5 Leanna G 7
    Margaret *List* Sarah P 14
    William *List*
McDONOUGH E. A. LL 6
    L. H. LL 6
MILES John W. Y 8
MOORE John GG 5 Mary E. GG 5
MORGAN Philip W 11
MORRISON Archibald EE 10,
    EE 11, EE 12, EE 13 Flora
    H 10 Marry M. EE 11
    Rachel EE 10, EE 12
MYERS Catherine K 5
    William K 5
OREM Nathanel J 16
ORME Archibald D 2 Etta D 2
    Robert S. G 3
ORRISON Elizabeth V 8
    William D. V 8
PARSON S. J. LL 7 T. M. LL 7

POTTERFIELD Jacob I 5 Samuel
    AA 4 Johannes *Pile*
RICHARDSON M. I. S 21
    Rev. X. J. *Pile*, S 21
RICKARD George BB 6
RICKERT George BB 5
ROLLER Conrad EE 1, EE 2
    John *Pile*
ROPP Rachel Q 2 Samuel Q 2,
    W 14
RUSE Edward S. J 7
    Henry NN 11, PP 9
    Sarah NN 11
RUST James W. H 11, V 10
    Margaret V 10
SCHAEFFER Jacob Q 18
SHAFER Adam BB 11 Emma C.
    RR 14 John H. RR 14
SHAFFER Joseph B. P 9
    Susan P 9
SHEWMAKER Catharine II 18
    Simon II 18
SHUMAKER Simon II 19
SIMONS Edward UU 9, UU 10
    Mary A. UU 9 Mary Ann
    UU 10
SLATER Catharine LL 2 George
    J 7, U 31 Jacob J 2, LL 2
    John FF 2, X 2 Margaret
    S 16, S 17 Samuel W. K 1,
    K 4 William S 16, S 17
SMITH Job AA 8 Lydia AA 8
    T. CC 5
SNOOTS Anna J. M 5 John M 5
SPEAKS Charles C. Z 1
    Mary E. M 6 Richard M 6
    Sarah Ann Z 1
SPINKS Amie G 9 Lizzie G 9
    Mamie G 9 Mary G 9
SPRING Casper BB 18
    Charles W. TT 16 Elias
    P 12 Laura J. TT 16
STONE Elizabeth RR 3, RR 4,
    RR 5 Frederick *List*
    Samuel RR 3, RR 4, RR 5
STONEBURNER *List* C. E. L 18
    Catherine M 4 Frederick
    OO 2 J. C. L 18 Peter M 4
STOUTSENBERGER John P 3
    Mary K 1 Samuel K 1,
    KK 18, KK 20
STUCK F. F. U 8, U 9, U 10
    Jane U 8, U 9, U 10

SWANK Mary CC 11 Philip
    CC 11, EE 14
TRITAPOE Charles L 3 L. A. L 3
    Samuel CC 14
    Sarah F. CC 14
VICKERS Catherine U 14
    Charles CC 16 Edward F.
    CC 16 Eunice L. CC 16
    J. T. EE 20 L 27 James H.
    CC 16 John T. CC 16
    John G. CC 16 Mary G.
    CC 16 Rachel EE 20
    Richard L 27 Samuel
    CC 16 Sarah AA 5
    Susannah CC 16
    Thomas H. CC 16
    William AA 5, CC 16,
    T 13, U 14
VINCEL George G 5 John Sr.
    W 15 Louisa J 14, R 3
    Luther H. TT 15 Philip
    R 3 Solomon J 14
VINSEL John A. V 4
VIRTS Leah PP 1, PP 4
    Marietta L 24 Michael
    FF 5 Peter *List* N 13, PP 1,
    PP 4 W. Q 8
    William H. L 24
VIRTZS John KK 1 Peter KK 2
WALMAN John II 8
WALTMAN W. *List* Elias II 6
    Elizabeth II 6 Imanuel
    KK 12 Jacob Sr. II 7 Jacob
    II 11 Jacob Sr. II 12 Jacob
    KK 13 John KK 10
WENNER J. W. Q 14, R 12 John
    N 17 Jonathan K 21
    Jonathan A. K 21 L. Q 14,
    R 12 Mary C. K 21
WHITE Maria K 9 William K 9
WIARD Jonathan I 14
    Michael EE 16
WIAT Ann J 13 Emma I 13
    Jonathan J 13
WILLIAMS Amelia KK 24 H.
    S. *Pile* X 14 Israel N 1,
    O 1, KK 24, X 11 Joseph J.
    F 11, F 12 M. A. *Pile*
    Permelia O 1 Sarah A.
    P 13 Sophia C. F 11
    T. K. P 13
WILT Daisy E. W 22 J. F. W 22
WINE Jacob X 1

WINSEL Elizabeth U 5
    George R 2 Louisa R 4
    Philip R 4, U 5
WIRE George N 21, N 22 Sarah
    Ann N 21 Sarah L. N 22
WIRTS Christine DD 1, Y 4
    Peter DD 1 Y 4
WIRTZ Jacob T 3
WORDSWORTH Catherine
    EE 15 Lewis EE 15
WRIGHT A. S. *List* Margaret
    H. A. BB 21 S. J. *List*
    Samuel F. BB 21

www.ingramcontent.com/pod-product-compliance
Lightning Source LLC
Chambersburg PA
CBHW081202270326

41930CB00014B/3258